FOUR DAYS IN JULY

Also by Jim Huber

A Thousand Goodbyes
The Babes of Winter

FOUR DAYS IN JULY

Tom Watson,
the 2009 Open Championship,
and a Tournament for
the Ages

JIM HUBER

Thomas Dunne Books
St. Martin's Press ☙☙ New York

THOMAS DUNNE BOOKS.
An imprint of St. Martin's Press.

www.thomasdunnebooks.com
www.stmartins.com

Design by Level C

Scorecards courtesy of the R & A

Library of Congress Cataloging-in-Publication Data

Huber, Jim.
    Four days in July : Tom Watson, the 2009 Open Championship,
and a tournament for the ages / Jim Huber.
        p. cm.
    Summary: "The sports world watched breathlessly as Watson, just
shy of his 60th birthday and twenty-six years after his last Open title,
battled Father Time through four amazing rounds at Turnberry before
falling in a heartbreaking playoff to fellow American Stewart Cink. In
Four Days in July, Jim Huber mines his exclusive interviews with
Watson, caddy Neil Oxman, Cink (dubbed "The Man Who Shot Santa
Claus"), and many other luminaries to recount a heroic tale of resilience,
grit, and determination. This unforgettable story of the greatest links
player ever and his courageous quest will appeal to athletes of all
ages"—Provided by publisher.
    ISBN 978-0-312-66187-8 (hardback)
    1. British Open (Golf tournament) (2009 : Turnberry,
Scotland)   2. Watson, Tom, 1949–   I. Title.
    GV970.3.H83 2011
    796.352'66—dc22

                                                        2010054495

First Edition: May 2011

10 9 8 7 6 5 4 3 2 1

To Tom Watson,
who made an old world young again

CONTENTS

FOUR DAYS IN JULY

PROLOGUE

H e climbed out of bed for what must have been the tenth time that interminable Sunday night. Making certain he did not awaken his wife, he made his way silently onto the wide balcony off the bedroom of the hotel high atop a hill. Clouds hung low over the dark Irish Sea, but he could still see the outline of Ailsa Craig miles off the shoreline. A sliver of Scottish moon sprinkled shadows across the land.

The grandstands, empty and cold now, hid the 18th green from view, but there was no shrouding the huge, familiar old yellow scoreboard off to the left. He did not have to squint to read the names still at the top. He would see them imprinted on his intricate mind for all time.

Tom Watson rubbed his blue eyes. Visions hung where sleep refused. Sleep came fitfully most Sunday nights simply because of the leftover adrenaline that continued to course through his competitive system. But this was different. This was a night that would keep him awake for the rest of his life for a completely different reason.

He smiled. Sleep was overrated. You didn't have to sleep to dream.

As he stood on the balcony of the "Watson" suite at the Turnberry Hotel, those intense eyes roamed the unforgiving acreage across the road. Though the new moon offered very little in the way of illumination, the Scottish sky rarely reached its ultimate darkness this far north in the middle of summer. One way or the other, it didn't matter. It could have been the dead of winter and pitch-black. He knew every foot of the course so well that he could have closed his eyes and made the journey step by step, club by club, swing by swing.

It had, after all, been the scene of grand heroics in his professional golfing career.

And now, just hours ago, it had been the site of perhaps the most painful few minutes of his life. Jack Nicklaus said it best decades ago, he thought: All I'll take from this is that I lost.

But then again, this was so much more than just another defeat. This was a page very near the front of golf's history book torn out and shredded. This was an incredibly bitter fall just feet from the peak of one of the sports world's most un-approachable mountains.

He shook his head. Hundreds had slapped his back so hard there would be bruises. Thousands, tens of thousands, had come to tears. Millions would say they were inspired.

By second place.

He was not a man to live in the past. As in all sports you can't play golf that way. To be successful, you must learn early how to put aside your mistakes and look forward to the next shot, the next round, the next tournament. In a sport where batting .100 usually gets you into its Hall of Fame, looking backward will soon destroy whatever career you might have had. Watson won just 15 percent of the events he entered on the PGA Tour over forty seasons but was easily one of the most decorated players in the game's history, always with his eyes on the near horizon.

And yet, Tom Watson knew in the dark hours of this Scottish morning in July 2009 that he would be given no chance to forget what had just happened. What he had managed over the past four days, no matter the outcome, was a standard few, if any, would ever rise to. Who would even try? he wondered.

He stretched with his strong freckled hands clasped in the pit of his back. Had this been a dream? Had these four days been a seventy-six-hole aberration? He had risked early in the week telling the world how special he felt here. And then he had gone out and played like it. He had put together a game plan and by damn followed it nearly to perfection.

Had all of this just happened? Had he really just taken his own private miracle right to the edge of completion? And had he proved to a gaping world that age did not need to be a factor, not in this particular championship, not in this particular country?

Judging from the avalanche of emotion throughout the weekend, no, he would never be able to put this behind him.

1

THE DREAM FACTORY

It was midmorning on Monday, July 13, 2009. The wind off the Irish Sea gnawed at my ears as I huddled on the makeshift driving range. While the Ailsa Course at Turnberry was being used for the 138th Open Championship, the Kintyre Course—the resort's second eighteen—had been turned into parking lots, the television compound, hospitality areas, and the major range.

Even with the partially filled grandstands guarding my back, the wind, a regular visitor, still managed to find its entrance and make the day far colder than its announced 52 degrees.

I had finished shooting a feature to be used during Turner Broadcasting's coverage of the Open later in the week and decided to wander the range for a while, picking up bits of gossip, saying hello to old friends, watching new swings.

The driving range can be an awkward place for an outsider, and thus a delicate balance must be struck. It is, after all, an "office" of sorts, and while amateurs use a driving range to warm up tense muscles and somehow find a swing that will work, professionals use it the week of a tournament to groove perfection.

The mood varies dramatically from the beginning of the week straight through to Sunday afternoon. You can actually feel the concentration rise to a peak as the first round draws nigh and dwindles thereafter. Early in the week, the pros use the range as a test center, asking their caddies to stand behind them to make certain the plane of their swing is correct and their alignment proper. Some may not have played in several weeks and so it is a time for rearrangement. Gadgets, yellow stakes, props of all kinds guide their shoulders, their feet, their eyes. Occasionally, a caddie will stand behind his pro with a video camera and, after several swings, they will huddle over the small screen to check the results.

It is where dreams are put to work.

By Thursday morning as the first round dawns, they have their swings down to a science and use the range as a finishing school. On Friday, depending on how they played the first day, they rework. There can be a sense of desperation as they seek hurried answers.

Come the weekend, the players who arrive on the range early are those who only barely made the cut, and thus there tends to be a bit of acceptance, an "oh, well" kind of approach. Later in the morning, the contenders gather in full serious mode.

Early Sundays, the driving range can be nearly desolate. The also-rans use it for a quick warm-up. The tension grows as the final tee times approach and those in the hunt come to the range to prime their games. All of this rarely varies from tournament to tournament, although the senses tend to be heightened at the major championships.

I have learned over the decades how to approach the range. Just as it is the golf professional's workplace, so in a peripheral way is it mine. I usually wait to make eye contact, first with the caddies and then with their pros, if at all. If they respond, I approach to chat. If they nod and go right back to work, I move on. It is a field of learning for me. Some days I leave with wonderful nuggets to use during telecasts; other days I wind up with an empty notebook.

I have friends who envy me the experience there.

"Ah, your swing has gotta be absolutely perfect," they say without warrant, "spending so much time with the pros."

I must admit it can be a lethal concoction. I can on occasion come away with a fresh new idea, something to do with the right knee or the left shoulder, the way the feet are pointed or the hands positioned. More often, however, it is a collection of ideas that wind up twisting me like a Coney Island pretzel.

On this particular Monday at Turnberry, with the big Fijian Vijay Singh parked to his right and Australia's Robert Allenby to his left, Tom Watson was hard at work. I don't know what made me stop and watch him practice. It certainly wasn't a hunch, couldn't have been a preconceived notion of what was to come in a few days. There was, instead, something about the way he went about his business that attracted me. And then, of course, there was the sense of watching history.

His work ethic throughout the decades is legendary. I had often heard the story his present caddie, Neil Oxman, tells of an afternoon outside Pittsburgh in 1978 before the PGA Championship.

"We were standing at the back of the range at Oakmont, above the bunker where Tom was practicing," recalls Oxman, who was caddying for another golfer at the time.

"Oakmont is a very long course and you were likely to have some really long bunker shots. Tom was hitting 4-woods and 5-woods out of the bunker. We were there for about two and a half hours, and in that time, Tom never left the bunker.

"Two and a half hours! It was unbelievable how hard he worked."

That work paid large dividends that week. The twenty-nine-year old Watson fought his way into a sudden-death playoff, only to lose the PGA to John Mahaffey, one of forty-six top-ten finishes in major championships over Watson's career.

And despite the fact that Watson was now within weeks of turning sixty, he maintained that same dedication. No small irony that he was parked in the slot on the range next to Singh, who is known as one of the hardest workers on the Tour. Theirs would be a good duel.

My back against the wind, I watched Watson go about his business. Neil Oxman was a few yards behind him, wiping down grips and scrubbing grooves. Occasionally, he would wander to the table to the right of the range and pick up another bucket of Titleist balls.

On a professional driving range, each manufacturer provides practice balls for their men, the same brand they use on the golf course, Titleist, Bridgestone, Callaway, Srixon, Nike, TaylorMade, etc. The range workers who collect the balls during the day must then separate the brands to be used again. Each different ball, to men at this level, has its own feel, and they believe it is important to practice with what they play with.

Watson used the new Titleist Pro V1x that morning, though the balls in his own bag were a variety of Titleist designed two years before. Like his clubs and shoes and gloves and caps, he is a creature of well-worn habit. The older ball, the Pro V1, seemed to have a better feel to him. He liked the way it came off his club face. He grudgingly settled on the range for the newer model.

For a long moment on this blustery Monday, he raised his head and, like an old hunting dog, sniffed the wind. He knew this golf course well. After all, one of his five Open Championships had come here in high drama thirty-two years before and he had won a Senior British Open here just six years ago. This would be his seventh competition on this remarkable property along the western elbow of Scotland. He knew how the wind worked here, no matter whether it came off the water from the southwest, as it normally did, or reversed itself and rumbled over the hilltops from the east. Sometimes, it even changed midround, and he knew how to handle that, too.

He knew how to let it be his friend. There were men on this very driving range, Open rookies, who had never played on a course like Turnberry in their lives, never had the pleasure (or frustration) of a links experience. But Tom Watson, oh, my, it is said he is the greatest links player of all time, better than Old Tom Morris or his son Young Tom, better even than Harry Vardon, who won more Opens than anyone else in history. While some on the range were newcomers at this, Watson had played 148 competitive rounds in both the Open and the Senior British and more than three times that many practice rounds. So, as some men were about to face the intricate task for the very first time, here was a man who had played more than 450 rounds on links courses in the United Kingdom.

When Tom Watson sniffed the wind, you took notice.

Satisfied that it was gusting from the southwest, he took the 18-degree Adams Hybrid, one of two hybrid clubs in his bag these days, set it down neatly behind the Titleist, and with a crisp, efficient motion that hasn't changed a whole lot in forty years, sent the ball whistling toward the back of the range. As it rose and rode the wind, Watson kept his pose, frozen in time, until he watched the ball land 230 yards or so away and roll out. He didn't move until it stopped.

Then he did it again.

And again.

I watched the club nearly reach parallel on the backswing, his hands so high, his head so still, and thought, "My goodness, what a physical marvel this man still is." As age takes its unfair hold on golfers, their swings usually become shorter, their hips locked in stern refusal. Not Tom Watson.

He was deep in concentration, readying his game, when, out of the corner of an eye, he spotted an old friend and adversary making his entrance onto the range. Nick Faldo, the Brit who included three Opens among his six career major titles, strode earnestly toward an opening. His son Matthew, who was caddying for him that week, carried a large bag with the presumptuous but altogether accurate name "Sir Nick Faldo" stitched into the black leather. Knighthood had been conferred on the controversial player by Queen Elizabeth II nearly a month ago to the day. The official investiture, however, would not come for another four months, yet he had been quick to claim the title, anyway.

A sharp gleam twinkled in Watson's eyes and he quickly bent to his knees and bowed deeply in an I'm-not-worthy welcome.

"Oh, Sir Nick!" he exclaimed. "Sir Nick has arrived!"

It was probably what every other golfer had wished *he* had done but lacked either the seniority or the cojones. Faldo drew great admiration among his fellow players but little adoration, his flinty personality seeming to rub most of them very wrong.

Faldo tossed Watson a knight's wave and, almost embarrassed, stopped for a few words and moved on. Watson turned, winked at his caddie, and went back to work, his missiles once again piercing the crisp morning air. The moment of frivolity was now long gone.

———

"Something, eh?"

I turned and realized that Mark O'Meara was standing alongside me watching Watson. How long he had been there, I hadn't a clue. The former Open and Masters champion, now a member of the Champions Tour with Watson and the rest of the over-fifty set, shook his head.

"Guy can still play, can't he?"

I nodded and smiled. *Perhaps in his dreams.*

Surely this would be yet another two rounds and out for Watson. The old guy hadn't done better than a tie for tenth in the Open in two decades. Why, this century alone, he had missed three cuts and hadn't even started in two other Opens.

And he was playing his first Open on a new left hip, put in place just eight months before.

O'Meara smiled as though he had been reading my thoughts. "Believe me, he can still play."

The wind suddenly shifted and roared head-on. I nestled deeper into my jacket and left the old man to his work as I walked down the line to the man who surely would be the story of the week.

Tiger Woods had arrived.

2

A GOOD BET

Jeremy Kavanagh was windblown and still a bit wet from his first practice round over the demanding Ailsa Course that Monday as he stood in the players' lounge and scanned the practice sheet for the next day. Players had the privilege of signing up at whatever time and with whomever they wished for their practice rounds. There, mid-Tuesday morning, was the makings of a dream. Just two simple, common names, but to the lanky twenty-nine-year-old British journeyman who had qualified for his very first Open Championship, they might as well have been Ben Hogan and Bobby Jones.

Norman.

Watson.

Kavanagh, who had been working construction with his brother's building firm while the Open was being played in 2008, looked first left and then right. No one was watching. No one to laugh at the audacity. He carefully took a pen—not a pencil, nothing that could be erased—and made it one of the most lopsided threesomes in golf history.

Norman.

Watson.

Kavanagh.

"Why not?" thought the man from Stoke Park in Buckinghamshire. "Some of their magic might rub off."

Heart strumming, he quickly changed clothes and joined a friend thirty-five minutes along the coast road from Turnberry for an afternoon at a soggy, dangerous layout called the Ayr Racecourse, not far from where he was sharing a little room for the week with another pro. Ayr Racecourse is one of Scotland's premier tracks, hosting horse races year-round, but on this particular day, it would make headlines for all the wrong reasons.

The golfers arrived in time for the third race, a seven-furlong handicap featuring a dozen Thoroughbreds over the turf. Jeremy Kavanagh stepped to a betting window and perused the lineup. He was still tingling with the thought of the holy practice round the next morning when he saw a 12–1 entry called Whaston. The irony grabbed hold and he quickly put £5 of his hard-earned cash on the James Bethell–trained horse.

What immediately followed was a moment in time that would settle into the collective memories of those watching, in horror, for all time.

On the straight coming out of the home turn, a stretch of grass some of the jockeys in the two earlier races that day had derisively likened to an "ice patch" because of its slippery condition, a horse named Balwearie lost its footing and fell. In a terrifying split second, six more tumbled over him. A fortnight of heavy rain and an additional watering by the ground crew had made that portion of the track nearly unmanageable. Amazingly, only Balwearie among the horses was injured, suffering a broken jaw, and only two of the jockeys were slightly hurt.

Sensing danger, the Irish-born bay gelding called Whaston had danced its way through the ice patch and was long gone when the pileup occurred.

Whaston, at 12–1 with jockey Graham Gibbons flogging him and Jeremy Kavanagh cheering him on, won easily. The young golfer felt inordinately guilty, having witnessed the carnage while his own bet was galloping easily, safely home.

The winner went nearly unnoticed to most everyone else, however, as the accident drew furious headlines of course mismanagement and woeful conditions. The rest of the day's race schedule was canceled, a bit late in many minds. Kavanagh, however, had eyes only for the winner and hurried to cash in his ticket.

The next morning at Turnberry, a seriously nervous Kavanagh met his practice partners on the first tee and introduced himself. Greg Norman was pleasant but busy with his own game. Tom Watson chose to hang back and walk the first fairway with the young lad, who promptly told him the story of his misspelled namesake at the races twenty hours before.

Ironically, even the owners of the horse had misspelled its intended name. Clarendon Thoroughbred Racing syndicate names all of its horses after local villages or towns. Whashton is a tiny stop in North Yorkshire on the northeast coast of England where the syndicate trains, but when Sally Bethell made the official entry, she left out the second *h*.

And so Whashton became Whaston and, in Kavanagh's eyes, became Watson. Tom Watson, as is his manner, flashed that gap-toothed grin of his and chuckled.

"Maybe that name's got a lucky ring to it this week."

———

The name Watson has had a very Scottish ring to it since the first week Tom Watson ever set foot in the land. His initial journey to the home of golf came in 1975 for the Open held at the brutish and unforgiving Carnoustie, an old track on the east coast.

"We stayed at a little house in Monifieth [just down the road from Carnoustie]," he told John Huggan of the *Scotsman*, "and the whole week, the neighbors were very respectful of our privacy. Then on the last day they couldn't contain themselves any longer. That morning, a little girl from next door knocked on our front door and said, 'Here, this is for good luck.' I could hardly understand her. But she gave me a piece of heather, white heather, wrapped in foil. I put it in my bag and, sure enough, I won. That evening, it seemed like the whole neighborhood came by. My love affair with the Scottish people had begun."

It is incredibly rare that a first-timer manages to win the Open, given the valuable nature of experience on links courses. Ben Hogan did it at Carnoustie in 1953 and, that done, never returned. Watson found the same magic twenty-two years later on the same layout, but instead of forsaking the Open à la Hogan, he began a love affair with the championship that would last the rest of his days.

Still, it took words from a golfing legend to get Watson through that initial encounter.

"There wasn't much wind the first three rounds, very little rough, and I had my game plan," recalls Watson a generation later. "But before the last round, I went to Byron Nelson and asked for his advice."

A remarkable lifelong relationship with one of the game's true pioneers and one of its grandest citizens was in the early stages at that time. When Watson was troubled with his game or simply needed a wise old brain to pick, he would visit Lord Byron at Preston Trail Golf Club in Dallas. They would take a golf cart and drive to the far end of the range and sometimes not even get out, just sit and talk for hours.

Once in a while, Watson would take a club and go through the motions, inviting Nelson's guidance. Watson's father in the beginning, and Stan Thirsk, the pro at Kansas City Country Club later on, were the only others allowed to tinker with young Tom's immaculate game. But there was something about Byron Nelson—the soft Texas twang, the kind eyes, the generations of experience—that made the invitation easy.

One afternoon, they worked on Watson's short game. Watson would hit a few balls, then Nelson would take a club and show him how he might improve. The club pro at Preston Trail in those days was a man named Bob Goetz, who took photographs of the session. He had the film developed immediately and showed the pictures to Nelson the next day.

"Look how much better your club position is," Goetz said to Nelson, "than Tom's."

"Well, Bob," said Byron Nelson with his typical bashful understatement, "I *was* a pretty good player in my day."

Nelson, whose record of eleven straight PGA Tour victories in 1945 may never be broken, was working American television at Carnoustie when Watson came to him for help.

"He said something very specific," Watson told me about their conversation in 1975. "He said for the first time the winds are going to blow and scores are going to go up. Be patient and settle for par if you want to win this golf tournament. I kept it in mind the whole round. I made even par my goal that final round, and it was good enough. Great lesson, one that's carried me all these years later."

He won in an eighteen-hole playoff with Jack Newton, a brash, hard-living Australian who was so surprised to be in the playoff that he told the media, "First thing I have to do is cancel a pro-am I'm supposed to play in Dublin tomorrow. Then, I guess, get drunk again."

A 1st-tee comment from the gallery could have rattled Watson before the playoff that Sunday. "Don't let this bother you," someone yelled at him, "but this one's for America."

Watson laughed and then followed Nelson's advice again, shooting a smooth, error-free 71 in a continuous downpour that additional day for the improbable victory, thus beginning one of the most remarkable careers in major golf history.

"Another authentic American hero was born out of the gloom and crusty old atmosphere of golf on the linksland of Britain," Dan Jenkins wrote in *Sports Illustrated* the following week. "In a playoff for the British Open . . . , young Tom Watson finally became a champion, a new person, and one hellacious player."

It took a bit longer for his love affair with the Scottish game to flower. Like almost everyone who first comes to this land, including such greats as Bobby Jones and Sam Snead, he was initially perplexed and even infuriated at its vagaries.

Even the incomparable Jack Nicklaus, with three Opens among his eighteen major victories, had a tough time growing to love the links game.

"I don't mind the odd visit to play in British tournaments," he told the U.K. version of *Golf Illustrated* in 1962, "but if I had to play on your courses all season, it would drive me crazy. Golf is quite difficult enough without having to compete with rock-hard greens, and all kinds of humps and bumps in front of them."

He learned, as did Watson. Like Scotch whiskey, links golf is an acquired taste.

The very first hole Watson ever played in Scotland, he remembers hitting his drive right down the middle of the fairway and he exclaimed to Huggan, "We lost the ball! Lost the ball! Finally, I looked in this little pot bunker 50 yards off line and there it was! Boy, was I mad!"

For a man so frustrated in his links infancy, he soon learned to take advantage of this unique style of golf. Of his five Opens and three Senior British Opens, seven occurred in Scotland. Is there any better reason for a man's eyes to sparkle wide as he sets foot again on the auld sod than that kind of pedigree? Despite his age, he knew that this style of golf could play right into his hands.

"The links game is a ground game," explains former Masters and U.S. Open champion Billy Casper. "In America, it is an air game. As a guy gets older, he relies more on the ground than the air because he doesn't hit it as far. Of course, Tom hasn't lost all that much distance yet. But if you have a course with conditions and features set up for an older player, well, who better . . . ?"

Who better than Watson indeed? Though he had not been competitive in the Open in two decades, he was re-turning to his adopted land where the most astonishing dreams can apparently come true. And though he hadn't played a competitive round in weeks, Watson felt amazingly good about his game going into Turnberry.

"Usually," his caddie Neil Oxman told me, "Tom will say, 'Ox, I'm trying to do this, I'm trying to do that, I'm trying to get my hands here, I'm trying to work the ball this way, watch me, will you?' But there was none of that at Turnberry. He never said anything like that. He was just so confident."

"I arrived on Monday," Watson recalls, "and played a practice round right away. I was hitting the ball very well but wasn't putting really well. Tuesday, I changed my putting, started getting the ball rolling where I wanted it to go.

"It was just a minor thing, a little change, but I just had to find something that was working. This happened to work pretty well and the results were good."

Better than good.

3

A THOUSAND TO ONE

Chris Card, tall, with a perpetual smile, loved the look of surprise on the golfers' faces when he welcomed them to Turnberry.

"Last thing anybody expects," he said with a laugh, "is an American accent greeting them."

The forty-year-old professional had worked for years at Innisbrook Resort and Golf Club near Tampa, Florida, before moving to Landfall in Wilmington, North Carolina. He had been Turnberry's director of golf for only two months prior to the Open, a daunting challenge, to say the least. A bit like being named Director of Snow in the days leading up to a Winter Olympics. It was good that he delayed moving his wife and twin six-year-old daughters to this magical land until well after the Open was over, for his were eighteen-hour days. He made it a point, not only for himself but also for each member of his staff, to greet every one of the 156 men in the Open field each day and make certain they felt at home.

"I remember shaking hands with Tom," he recalls, "and thinking about the legend standing in front of me. Now, I've worked professional tournaments over the years, but still, here was *the* Tom Watson.

"I specifically watched him on the range and then followed him for a dozen or so holes during a practice round early in the week, and I must admit it was kinda eerie. He was so cool, so calm. I thought, 'Look at him, there is something going on there, something in his air.'

"He seemed genuinely happy to be here, so comfortable. He made sure he said hello to everyone, no matter their rank."

Card allowed himself a private thought early that week. "Wouldn't it be neat?" he said to himself. And then he laughed out loud. Wouldn't it be outrageous?

———

There are upward of twenty-five hundred Ladbrokes in the United Kingdom and Europe, twenty-five hundred dealers in dreams. Legal gambling has thrived everywhere in Great Britain, from giant metropolises to bare bumps in tiny roads since the Betting and Gaming Act of 1961.

If you drive the A77 from Turnberry along the sea toward the ancient fishing port of Girvan, take the second exit off the Knockcushan roundabout onto Dalrymple Street. Two blocks down on your right, with the familiar bright red sign hanging over the sidewalk, is the village's only gambling palace.

The odds for the ill-fated and tragic race at Ayr Racecourse earlier that afternoon were still awkwardly handwritten on the wall in black on white. You could also place a wager on the Ashes, one of the most celebrated Test cricket matches in the world, which would begin in London this very week. Could England finally gain a foothold against the dominating Australians? Football, cricket, rugby, even cycling—all had a price in this humble shop.

And there amidst it all was a list of 156 names, some household, some not even in their own. The field for the first Open championship to grace the nearby Turnberry Ailsa Course in fifteen years, only the fourth in its history, was a mixed bag. From Jaco Ahlers of South Africa to Azuma Yano of Japan. From sixteen-year-old amateur Matteo Manassero of Italy to fifty-nine-year-old Tom Watson of the United States, the five-time Open champion.

Tiger Woods—or as longtime first-tee announcer Ivor Robson simply trills in his high-pitched, familiar lilt, "From USA, Tiger Woods"—was far and away the betting favorite. It almost made no sense placing a wager on him, unless you simply wanted a piece of history. Ladbrokes had him at 9–4.

Watson and Manassero, the aged bookends who would wind up playing together the first two rounds, were each 1,000–1, as was Jeremy Kavanagh. One thousand to one tends to be a road to nowhere, along which are dumped the afterthoughts, but these were better odds than a few other books, which had Watson as high as 2,500–1.

The bald American Stewart Cink was 125–1, typifying a

career that had flown quietly under the radar for the most part. If anyone had an early inkling about him this particular week, no one said so. He was simply there, as he always was, like his odds, somewhere in the middle of it all.

Calum Imray, short, chubby, and with a brogue thicker than his waist, was leaning on the counter in Girvan, reading a football fan magazine when the bell rang over the front door. He had worked the day shift at this shop for nine years and thus had never experienced an Open in the neighborhood. Business had been slow, but with fans pouring into the area for the Open, he expected it to start picking up as the week progressed. Especially the Americans. They seemed to love the novelty of legal wagering.

He never took his eyes off the magazine, however, as a sturdy old man entered. The tall, gaunt visitor rubbed his right shoulder unconsciously as his eyes sought out the Open Championship board.

It was a shoulder that had sagged under a thousand heavy golf bags over the decades, and they were eyes that could still gauge yardage from the middle of a fairway to a whipping yellow flag 248 yards away, give or take an inch, without once giving in to a book or a sprinkler head.

And he didn't have to look long at the board: ten from the bottom, 146 from the top.

The thought never crossed his old mind what *his* man would think, him wagering on another. It was a thought that had simply hung with him for a few hours now. There the man had been, a fairway across, and what a sight he was. The old

familiar steady swing, the strict pose at the finish as he studied
his result, the slight smile across the weathered, freckled face.
It was almost as if the guy knew something none of the rest of
us knew. Tough, focused, demanding even though it was just a
practice round, sorta like the Watson of old, and the caddie
shook his head at the thought. Many's the time he and his
man had been paired with Watson over the decades of his
Open history and nobody, just plain nobody, could look the
old bitch, Mother Nature, in the eye and win that stare-
down like him.

The caddie made it a habit, every week on the European tour, to stop by a Ladbrokes or a William Hill and place
a quid or five on his own man. It seemed to make him work
just that much harder. Never did he bet against his bag, and
the way he saw it, he wasn't doing that this week, either. He
just smelled something special. That look in Watson's eyes.

"Tenner on Watson to win."

"You sure?" cautioned Calum Imray, his magazine put
aside for the moment. It was a question he never, ever normally asked. It was, after all, their business, their money, and
if they wanted to throw it his way, so be it. But for this one
moment, he sought caution.

"Never sure," chuckled the caddie, "but let's just give it a
try, what say?"

Imray exchanged a receipt for the wager and shook his
head. Never know what's going through a gambler's mind.

4

RIDING IN THE LEAD CARRIAGE

July 15, 2005

It was a sun-splashed, windless Friday at St Andrews on the eastern wing of Scotland. Rarely are those adjectives used to describe the rough old layout generally known as the birthplace of golf.

Sun-splashed? Windless? Hardly.

Most days, as if to nurture its reputation, the wind off the sea howls across the stark and rugged land, knocking both men and their weapons off-kilter. Because there are no trees and few hillocks, there is nothing to get in its way as it barrels westward, often carrying salty spray with it. From the heavens or the seas, it is difficult to tell the water's origin as you burrow deep into your rain suit and wonder what in God's name possessed you to undertake such an adventure.

Somehow, however, the gods knew that on this particular day in the very middle of the first decade of the new century, the greatest of them all would be raising his hand in royal fashion and bidding his faithful farewell. And so the sky sparkled in a kind of splendor rarely experienced in those parts and the wind was a gentle caress as Jack Nicklaus made his way along the familiar last stretch of holes in his final Open round.

He had made up his mind to retire from Open competition several years before, but through some interesting ministrations, it was arranged that the great man would make that final walk at his favorite course in the world in 2005. Give him the familiar old red sleeveless sweater with a neat white shirt and black trousers and send him out one final afternoon for old time's sake. He had begun wearing a tan cap, but he had it off so many times in salute to the enormous crowds that he wound up simply carrying it most of the way.

A few months before the 2005 Open, R&A president Peter Dawson was asked what his organization was considering to honor Nicklaus.

"We've got a few things in mind," he said, "but I'm sure Jack Nicklaus would rather be remembered as a competitor than as a monument."

———

As Nicklaus passed the Old Course Hotel along the 17th fairway, fans hung out of windows and waved their teary goodbyes to the man considered the best who ever played the game. Even the giant South African Ernie Els, his round long finished, settled his elbows on his windowsill and watched the journey unfold below. If there were tears, he quickly wiped them away.

Nicklaus was paired the first two days with his good friend Tom Watson and the young Englishman Luke Donald, a tribute to battles past and to the young man who shared a Scottish banking endorsement with Nicklaus. Those in charge of putting together the first-round pairings at the Open always seem to take great delight in mixing and matching, as though they were throwing a great dinner party and were trying to decide who would make the best and liveliest partners.

There remained a bit of drama on this important Friday, as there always seemed to when he played. Nicklaus, with three Opens among his eighteen major championship victories, could still possibly make the cut and play the weekend. The loving crowds were desperately trying to will it. But when he bogied the 17th, the infamous Road Hole, he knew that his time on the Open rotation was over.

"After he putted out at 17," said Neil Oxman, "he came over and stood next to me and said, 'Ox, that was my last shot as a real golfer. The next shot will be my first as a ceremonial golfer.'"

And seconds later, with the faithful thousands literally hanging from the rooftops and out of windows and lining the tiny side street to the right of the fairway, Nicklaus stepped to the 18th tee and ripped his last Open drive.

Thus began the ceremony.

He and Watson and Donald stood for photographs on

the Swilken Bridge that splits the fairway. The caddies then joined them for more, all the while the thunder of the crowd gathering in intensity.

Nicklaus and Watson walked arm in arm down the fairway, tears streaming down their cheeks. Watson stepped back to allow Nicklaus his spotlight, and Jack took it.

Ironically, the previous morning, in the haze of a Scottish dawn, they had called for a moment of silence on these same grounds to honor those who had died in a terrorist bombing in London exactly a week before. The air shuddered and the land grew eerily quiet, as though not a soul stood within miles. Men paused, heads bare and bowed, at every green, in every fairway. Galleries shadowed them in a fearful silence.

These were tremulous times. The echoes of 9/11 still hung over the planet. Bali and Barcelona both had felt the wicked thunder. Now London. As golf fans made their way north to St Andrews the week of the bombings, a gathering of world leaders called the G-8 had already encamped at Gleneagles, just a few miles west of St Andrews. Heavily armed troops patrolled the bridge leading from Edinburgh over the Firth of Forth to Perthshire and on to the birthplace of golf.

Though perhaps the most elegant championship in all of golf, the Open took on a unique perspective the summer of 2005: the poignant end of the Nicklaus era paired with the proliferation of the most terrifying of times.

But a day after the moment of silence, that same air was thick with tremendous piercing cries as thousands honored one of their adopted sons. The fans were along the right side of the fairway and behind the 18th green while golfers of every country, every age, along with their families, lined the same fairway to the left and joined in the celebration.

Nicklaus and Watson were clearly moved.

"Tom's more of a sentimental old fool than I am," Nicklaus teased later. "He had more tears in his eyes than I did."

It was a moment that will last forever in the memories of those who watched. And certainly, it was one that taught Tom Watson another remarkable lesson in grace and style, something he already had in great abundance.

"I was grateful for that opportunity to play with Jack during his last two rounds," he said. "I had a chance to play with the greatest player who ever played the game. The golf world understood that he was something special in the game of golf. They appreciated Jack with their applause and cheers. He had earned that, and the people who knew the game, the people who go to the Open Championship and know the game so well, you take their cheers with a little bit more of an honest nature.

"They weren't cheering a celebrity, but they were cheering what they knew of Jack and what he represented throughout his career, especially at the Open."

Nicklaus finished that magical afternoon with a birdie at the closing hole, acknowledged the enormous gathering, bear-hugged Watson, and then made his way toward the old clubhouse. As he made his way up the steps, he spotted Peter Dawson.

"Hmmm," he whispered to Dawson as he shook his hand, "competitor rather than a monument. I like that."

July 16, 2009

From the very first of his seventy-six holes at the Open four years later in 2009, from the first wave of cheers at the opening tee to the outpouring at the last green four days later, Tom Watson felt this was to be something more than ceremony. With Nicklaus resigned from the Open, Watson knew he rode in the lead carriage at Turnberry. He heard the galleries crying, "Toom, Toom," in that familiar, unique style. He saw them standing in honor. He knew why and he responded in kind.

"I've always had the theory that if people acknowledge me, I acknowledge them," says Watson. "If I'm on a stage and give a great performance and they appreciate that, I then appreciate their applause and their cheers. Always been that way."

He and the galleries also knew that, with the new edict from the Royal and Ancient mandating a "use-by" date of age sixty, he had only this and the 2010 tournament— ironically back at St Andrews—left. And while he was polite about the ruling, others, some among his peer group and some decades younger, took umbrage.

"Since when does golf have age limits?" railed good friend and Champions Tour mate Andy Bean. "It's still an *open* championship and I just think that [putting an age limit on it] is just wrong."

"He said to me earlier this week, and I'm sure he said it

publicly," said England's young star Justin Rose, "that he wanted to win this championship so he can keep playing it.

"The greatest links player of all time deserves to play the Open as long as he wants, in my opinion. If I don't win, I'll certainly be rooting for Tom Watson."

Watson, however, whose relationship with the R&A had always been strong, publicly agreed with the edict.

"It's sensible," he said in a media session during Open week. "You have to give the young kids a chance to play, and that's the whole reason behind it. Get the old fogeys out of there and give the youngsters a chance to shine."

But behind the politically-correct statement was the thought that he shared with Rose. A victory at Turnberry, you see, would eliminate the mandate and give him an exemption for another ten years . . . taking him a few weeks shy of seventy. And honestly, deep within himself, Tom Watson, Old Tom, thought he had just as good a chance to win as anyone. If he used the word "special" once in regard to the week, he used it a hundred times and meant every letter.

As early as two weeks prior to Turnberry, Watson had said that his primary objective was not just to play well but to win, "to compete against the kids. I can still beat that golf course somehow."

On the eve of the opening round of the 138th Open, Watson received the first of several text messages from Barbara Nicklaus wishing him luck. Because her husband rarely texted anyone, she did the family correspondence. Watson texted her right back.

"I told her, 'You know, we really miss you over here,'" he said, "and I meant it. It's not the same without Jack playing in the tournament."

There was also something different about this Open for Tom Watson, something intimate and powerful.

"I felt going in that I could win," he recalled to me months later. "I really did have a legitimate chance of winning the tournament. I was playing well. I think I mentioned it to the press. I was playing well and they asked the age-old question, 'Do you think you can win?' and I said of course I can. That wasn't a toss-aside answer. I really meant it.

"The last time I felt that way? I can't remember. Maybe in 1994 right there at Turnberry. I really felt then that I could win, but my putting let me down. Yeah, it had been a decade or two since that feeling. It's the feeling of excitement and expectations, of positive thoughts. It was a feeling that I *very well could win* if I hit it well and continued to do what I had done in the practice rounds."

Game on.

5

THE OPENING ROUND: A GENTLE LADY

Thursday, July 16, 2009, dawned calm and brilliant over the southwestern coast of Scotland, the weather almost identical to that magical day on the opposite side of the country at St Andrews four years earlier when Tom Watson had been Jack Nicklaus's wingman on the road to history.

The huge rock called Ailsa Craig, which looms eleven miles off Turnberry's edge in the Firth of Clyde, which becomes the Irish Sea, was crystal clear and the conditions for the first round of the 138th Open were perfect for scoring.

Two miles in circumference and a thousand feet above the water, the hulking granite island was once a flourishing quarry that produced rock for such things as curling stones and chapel floors. It is populated now only by gannets and puffins. The local adage about Ailsa Craig offered to every golfer stepping foot on either of Turnberry's courses is always good for a laugh: "If you can't see Ailsa Craig, it's raining. If you can see it, it's going to rain."

This day, however, proved that pleasantly apocryphal. Even in the middle of the night, the summer skies were alive, streaked blood-red and black, as George Brown, Turnberry's veteran greenkeeper (or, as the Brits call it, golf courses and estates manager), gathered his entire grounds crew together in the shed near the driving range. They had gone through a tumultuous winter and spring, the course closed to traffic as renovations were being made. Now they all were on the verge of the payoff. The Open that had once seemed so very, very far away was now just beyond a gentle sunrise.

"I am so proud of you all," Brown said in his classic Scottish brogue at three in the morning, just a few hours before the opening tee shot. "For everything that each and every one of you did over the past months, this is the pinnacle. We are here, at last, and it's thanks in large part to you."

A cheer rocked the huge shed and echoed down the road toward where, in no time at all, the world would finally come calling. The first tee time was 6:30 with Paul Broadhurst, Michael Campbell, and Mark Calcavecchia as the grand marshals of this eagerly anticipated parade.

The ninth game of the day had Tom Watson, Sergio Garcia, and Matteo Manassero off at 8:09 and, in truth, if there was any interest initially in this grouping, it was to see if Garcia could somehow finally win a major after so many years of promise. It would also allow the world a glimpse of the promising youngster from Verona who had qualified for the Open by winning the British Amateur a few months previous. Watson seemed along for a sentimental ride.

Though his hair remained a dark and youthful auburn, Watson was a study in varying shades of gray that morning. A pearl, white, and black argyle sweater covered a blue shirt. Gray slacks slid over black golf shoes. A black cap adorned with his equipment maker Adams's name written in white across the front covered his head. It would be gently lifted often over the next four days, responding to the vigorous cries at every hole from the appreciative galleries.

Like so many in his profession, Watson rarely took his cap completely off in acknowledgment, instead placing the thumb and forefinger of his right hand on the end of the bill and tilting it skyward just enough to reveal the glistening eyes and warm smile below. At the end of each day, as he heard the tumultuous roars, he would remove it and bow slightly in courtly deference.

The silver-haired man of introductions, Ivor Robson, standing off to the side, raised his microphone into the crisp Thursday morning air. Though recognizable chiefly because of his decades of work at the Open, the dapper Scotsman is also the official first-tee host of the PGA European Tour.

There may not be anyone else in sport like him. From the very first tee time in the wee small hours of the morning to the very last one perhaps ten hours later, he never moves, never leaves his post. In the best and worst weather, in the harshest heat and the most familiar windblown chill, with rain sometimes pelting sideways, he stands guard at the first tee, welcoming each and every player in the field through four rounds of play. Though there is usually a portable john nearby, he never takes advantage, and he is asked every year how he manages that.

"Nothing in, nothing out." He smiles at the line he has used since his first Open duties in 1975—the year Watson won his first at Carnoustie. He eats a sandwich and downs a bottle of mineral water early the evening before, and after that . . . nothing. He claims to lose about fourteen pounds throughout the week.

His job is not simply to announce the players. He checks each player's golf ball to make certain it is sanctioned, verifies the pronunciation of the player's name if he comes to him unknown, and checks the familiar large Rolex clock nearby to make sure the player is not late.

In the midst of Robson's third Open, with the microphone at Turnberry in 1977, Mike Corcoran, who wrote *Duel in the Sun*, asked him if he was ever nervous executing his duties.

"Only I and my laundry know." Robson smiled in return. Like his introductions, he is a pleasant man of very few but well-rehearsed words.

On this lovely morning, Robson greeted the threesome and their caddies and announced them to the gathered fans. It was near the beginning of his usual marathon day, and he managed a polite smile.

As Watson stepped to the tee, he went to Robson and

shook his hand. "Good morning, Ivor," he said with an imp-
ish grin, "and when's your first break?"

"Oh, in about nine and a half hours," said Robson with
only the slightest of smiles. It was a conversation they had
managed quite often over the decades.

The 1st hole, appropriately called Ailsa Craig, is a 354-
yard par 4, your initial lesson in links management. Though
it would be tempting for the average golfer to simply take a
driver and blast it toward the sea, men like Watson begin
strategizing before their very first swing.

The primary key to playing successful links golf not only
at Turnberry but at any of the seaside layouts, aside from
judging the wind, is to avoid the plethora of fairway pot bunkers. And thus Watson used a 4-iron to slide his ball past the
bunker 220 yards down the left side. There was virtually no
wind at all that morning, a phenomenon that would continue
the entire round. (There was always a breeze, subtle and inviting, for you can rarely stand at the edge of any great body
of water and not feel *something* on your cheek, but never this
day the kind of real wind that can make the Open such a
vigorous challenge.)

"You have a bunch of choices on the 1st hole," recalls
Neil Oxman. "There are those four bunkers down the left
side. You can actually carry the last one, which is 310 yards,
if you're a big hitter, but most everybody plays short of the
first bunker."

Watson's initial drive through the avenue of bunkers was

perfectly placed, leaving him 126 yards to the front of the green, 138 to the hole itself. He chose a 9-iron, hit the shot hole high right, and made the 12-foot putt for birdie.

"You try not to get excited," says Oxman, "because you just don't wanna get goofy out there. But looking back, it was significant only in the fact that his name immediately went up on every leaderboard throughout the course and never left for four straight days."

It was not always at the very top, but it was there, a familiar old ghost haunting the field.

There is a great deal of feel when it comes to playing links golf, and so Watson's choice of clubs over the weekend would mean nothing in the American game. But for reference, this was his general yardage per club at the time:

driver: 255 yards

3-wood: 235

2-hybrid: 224

3-hybrid: 215

3-iron: 210

4-iron: 195

5-iron: 185

6-iron: 178

7-iron: 162

8-iron: 145

9-iron: 135

pitching wedge: 128

sand wedge: 95–100

Unlike many of the modern golfers, Watson carried only two wedges at Turnberry, choosing instead to round out the standard fourteen-club bag with hybrids. In contrast, there are tournaments where someone like Phil Mickelson will carry as many as four or five wedges. Watson, however, has developed the remarkable art of dialing up or down between his wedges, backing off to fit the yardage. The gap in yardage between his pitching wedge and sand wedge is the largest in his bag, so he has learned to play with the touch of a cat burglar.

The 2nd hole is called Mak Siccar (Make Sure), a 428-yard par 4 where, once again, the object is to stay out of the bunker on the right, which is 288 yards from the tee. It is the first chance a newcomer has of discovering just how relatively flat this landscape is; as you turn to the 2nd tee, there in the distance looms the famous lighthouse, easily a half mile away.

The second fairway rolls hard and is very narrow. There was the hint of a breeze in his face, which was the opposite of the prevailing winds, when he took the 2-hybrid and placed his ball in the middle of the fairway. With 191 yards to the pin, which was on the left side of the green, Watson's 6-iron shot went about 15 yards past the hole, and he 2-putted for par.

The course is laid out in a lateral design so the 3rd hole runs back toward the sea in the same direction as the first, a 489-yard par 4. It is called Blaw Wearie (Out of Breath), for usually the wind is dead in your face here.

For the first time, Watson used his driver and split the fairway, leaving himself 210 yards to the pin, which was on the left side of the green. His 4-iron shot landed about 20 feet short of the hole, and he drained the putt for his second birdie in his first three holes.

Ears were beginning to perk, minds tossing a bit. What a familiar sight, the name Watson atop the traditional old manual yellow leaderboards. Is it 2003 again and the battle of seniors here? Or, better yet, is it 1977? Are we in for another duel? The very thought brought slight laughter. This was, surely, for old time's sake and nothing more.

There is, on days and on courses such as this, a soft and gentle smell to the air that seems a luscious mixture of sea salt and heather, and so it was on this first day of the Open that men like Watson didn't so much walk the fairways as bask in the fragrance. It was Scotland and you could smell it and feel it and taste it.

It was one of the many things Watson enjoyed here, taking advantage of the entire experience, and so every once in a while you would see him raise his head a bit and offer a smile as though he had just remembered a good joke or a fond memory. The gentle nature of this particular day made that so much easier, for his mind was not being battered by a gale or soaked by a storm.

The 4th hole (Woe-Be-Tide) is the first of the four par 3s. The wind is usually in your face as you look toward Ireland, but the flag hung almost limp that Thursday. Watson had 145 yards to the front of the green, the pin just 9 yards on. He hit an 8-iron about 15 feet past the hole and 2-putted for par.

With the gentle breeze shifting a bit to his back at the par-4 5th hole, he used his driver and hit the ball 305 yards to the center of the undulating fairway. This hole is called Fin Me Oot, or Find Me Out, because there is much to be discovered in this undulating dogleg-left fairway.

The gallery grew in number and enthusiasm as the morning blossomed. It was far too early to give any thought whatsoever to the man's present or future; they were cheering instead his glorious past as he came their way. Scottish galleries have been primed for such celebrations since the days of the other Old Tom, and they treated their heroes like royalty.

With 188 yards left to the pin, Watson's 6-iron shot sailed past the hole to the back fringe of the green, which nestles in the sand dunes. A devilish downhill attempt with the putter left him with a tap-in for his par, and he and Oxman walked to the 6th tee standing 2-under par for the championship.

The 6th (Tappie Toorie, or Hit to the Top) is the longest of the par 3s, measuring 223 yards, and what there was of a wind was back in his face. He hit the 2-hybrid, the ball ending up about 25 feet pin high, and he 2-putted for par.

The 7th hole (Roon the Ben) is the only par 5 on the front nine, measuring 538 yards, and it fits quite nicely into the Watson history book. It was here on the final day of the 1977 Open that he reached it with two drivers and took two putts, using just two clubs out of his bag to get the birdie. He chose driver again, but for the first time, despite driving it 305 yards, the ball could not avoid the first fairway bunker on the right. He calmly took his medicine, chipped out, reached the green in 3, than 2-putted for par and moved on. Par, as he learned so many years ago at the feet of Byron Nelson, is always a good score at the Open.

The 8th hole is a par 4 measuring 454 yards. It's called Goat Fell, named after the tallest peak on the Isle of Arran, which sits just off the coast north of Turnberry. Watson chose a driver again, and this time his shot found the fairway. But from 148 yards, he missed the green on the left fringe and once again settled for a 2-putt par.

Appropriately called Bruce's Castle, the 9th hole is the first to take your breath away. There to the left sits the grand old lighthouse, built in 1873 amid the ruins of Turnberry Castle. It was there, the story goes, that Robert the Bruce was born, and the castle guarded the coastline until it was dismantled in 1310. The lighthouse still guides the way through the dangerous channel and distracts many a golfer on his or her way to the close of the first nine.

Watson stopped, rested a hand on his driver as he would a cane, and simply took in the grand beauty and history surrounding him. It was a view he had begun enjoying four decades before and it never seemed to change or grow old.

Much like him.

When he snapped out of his reverie, he chose a 3-wood off the tee on the rocky cliffs and watched the Titleist roll through the slim fairway and into the right rough. Wispy strands of fescue waved in the gentle breeze as he surveyed his options. He had 215 yards to the flag but wanted no part of that undertaking. His number instead was 185 yards, 2 yards shy of the front of the green. It was a links shot, pure and simple, hitting short and rolling onto the green. From 15 feet away, he 2-putted for another par and closed out his first nine holes at a 2-under par 33.

The 10th hole is a demanding 457-yard par 4 with bunkers right in the middle of the fairway, forcing you to go either right or left. It is called Dinna Fouter, or Don't Mess About. Watson chose a 3-wood and hit the ball short of the first bunker, which stands 276 yards out. He had 165 yards to the front of the green and another 10 to the hole. He hit a 6-iron stiff. The resulting 3-foot birdie moved him to 3 under par for the day, and the murmurs began in earnest, as if something memorable was riding the kindly zephyrs this pleasant July morning.

Some recalled Watson's heroics at this same hole in the 2003 Senior British Open, when he eagled it in the final round on his way to victory.

Six years later, heads in the huge media center rose, eyes squinted at the much-bigger scoreboard, smiles creased old knowing faces. They, especially, loved the idea of Watson in contention. Even though it surely would not hold up, it gave them a feel-good early-deadline story on this first day and would last until the real leaders came home.

"It was fun out there," recalls Oxman. "But again, I didn't wanna get too goofy. There was too much time left."

The 11th hole, called Maidens after a small caravan town just down the street from the resort, is the third par 3 of the day, a relatively short test at 175 yards. Though the measurements Watson and Oxman pay most attention to are to the front of the green, because you can't go pin hunting in links golf and live to tell about it, the par-3 numbers are precisely to the flag. Watson hit a 6-iron shot hole high and left, 2-putted for par, and moved on.

The 12th hole is a great test, a par 4 measuring 431 yards to the front of the green. Watson chose a driver and hit the ball 302 yards. Paired with the sixteen-year-old Manassero and the twenty-nine-year-old Garcia, Watson and the youngster matched each other in yardage off nearly ever tee, despite the forty-four-year difference in their ages. Garcia spent the day 25 to 30 yards in front of both of them. Just as age didn't matter, neither did distance. Watson beat Garcia that day by 5 strokes and Manassero by 6.

He had 131 yards to the front of the 12th green, 139 to the hole. His 9-iron shot ended up 14 feet to the left, and he rolled in the putt for his fourth birdie of the day.

To the right of the green rises a large mound. On top of it is a stately monument commemorating the airmen from the nearby base who were lost in the two world wars. Fans encircle the marble obelisk for a panoramic view of the 11th fairway, the 12th green, and the 13th tee box.

Watson stopped, as he always did, and stared up in silent honor, shuddering quietly at the thought of the grand sacrifices of the men who flew from what had been airstrips here decades ago. He had been touched by those who protected his freedom for as long as he could remember and tried to spend as much time with them as his schedule allowed.

He blinked his way back to the moment at hand and stared out over the final stretch of holes. There, sitting elegantly on the hill overlooking them, was the great hotel. Directly over the back entrance and the steps that lead down to the courses were the balcony and windows to his suite. He was headed home.

The 13th hole is a par-4, 410-yarder that requires more precision than most. There are three bunkers on the left side of the fairway and what the pros lovingly call "junk" all down the right. Junk is vegetation in which you could lose small children.

With a hint of breeze in his face, Watson's 2-hybrid tee shot landed in perfect position on the dogleg right, leaving himself 130 yards to the front of a long, diagonal, elevated green, one of only two holes on the course without greenside bunkers. The flag was another 25 feet from the left. Wisely,

Watson took an 8-iron 30 feet past the hole, then 2-putted for par. The hole is named Tickly Tap, reminding everyone to be gentle with the putts, for the slope of the green is legendary. He was that.

The 14th is a par 4 measuring 449 yards. Watson, at the top of the leaderboard at 4 under par, hit a 3-wood off the tee. It's called Risk-an-Hope, meaning you must be bold, but he was having none of that. He had 161 yards to the front, another 21 to the hole, and his 4-iron sent the ball into a greenside bunker. He managed to get it up and down for par, his scorecard remaining unblemished.

Called Ca' Canny, or Take Care, the 15th hole is the day's final par-3. Watson had 180 yards to the green's front, another 16 to the hole, and he blew a 5-iron shot nearly 40 feet past the hole. He 2-putted for par.

The 16th is a 455-yard par 4. As lunchtime began tolling and a near-sixty-year-old stomach began to grumble, its owner hit a perfect driver and had just 122 yards to the front of the green. The hole's name is Wee Burn, signifying Wilson's Burn, a meandering stream that fronts the green and rambles along its right side. Anything not on target finds the slope and carries down into the deep gorge. The flag was on 19 and Watson's 9-iron shot ended up hole high but at least 30 feet away. Once again, he 2-putted for par.

The 17th was one of the easiest holes all week, certainly playing right into Watson's hands. It's a 558-yard par 5 that usually plays downwind, as it did on Thursday. It's called Lang Whang or Long Whack, and he delivered. Watson's driver left his ball just 230 yards to the front of the elevated green, another 25 to the pin. He hit a 3-wood, the ball landing in the right-front fringe. It was a perfect placement—he had the entire length of the green to play his chip and run, which left him a tap-in birdie.

Tom Watson, holy smokes, now 5-under par going to the refurbished, much-tougher 461-yard par-4 finishing hole on a picture-postcard day at Turnberry. Could that be possible?

He chose a 2-hybrid at the 18th and stood just a few feet away from the marble marker that gives the hole's distance and its name.

DUEL IN THE SUN it reads, taking the visitor back thirty-two years to the drama that had unfolded on this very spot in the first Open Championship to grace this land.

Watson never looked at it.

His drive rolled through the dogleg left fairway into the light rough on the right, leaving him 180 yards to the front of the green. Any farther and his ball would have found some of the thickest gorse bushes on the course, just where Jack Nicklaus landed in the final round of their "duel" in '77. Nicklaus made such a remarkable recovery from the gorse that in the hours afterward, locals found the gash in the ground there and poured coins in it for good luck. Nicklaus's shot was only for show, however, as Watson tapped in his short birdie for the victory that day.

Now the flag was 22 feet to the right. He hit a 7-iron and the ball wound up 30 feet from the flag. Two putts and he posted one of the most remarkable first rounds in Open history. Never has a man of this age played so flawlessly for four and a half hours across one of the toughest pieces of landscape in all of golf.

The numbers were startling: out in 33, home in 32.

"It was just a perfect round of golf," recalls Oxman.

It seemed simple enough. The key to good rounds in any tournament is fairways and greens. And, as Oxman said, Watson was as close to perfect on the opening day as one could ask. He missed the fairway only twice, at the 9th, which he missed all four days, and the 18th. Hitting twelve out of fourteen fairways put him near the top of the 156-man field in that category by the end of the day.

He also hit fifteen of the eighteen greens in regulation, missing only the 5th, 8th, and 9th. Just as he struggled hitting the 9th fairway throughout the championship, so did he miss the long par-4 5th green all four days.

His scorecard at the end of that first day was immaculate. Birdies at 1, 3, 10, 12, and 17 against not a single bogey made for a brilliant 65, a magic number for Watson over his career. He put together a weekend's worth of 65s over this same Turnberry course on his way to the 1977 Open Championship. He and his ailing caddie Bruce Edwards sculpted a tear-stained 65 during the opening round of the 1993 U.S. Open at Chicago's Olympia Fields. And back here at Turnberry in the Open of 1994, he debuted with a 65 before his putter began letting him down again.

None, however, on the cusp of being a sexagenarian.

"She was defenseless today," Watson said afterward, true to his humble form. "It was an easy test, if there is such a thing at the Open."

While it was a step back in time for the thousands of fans who lined Watson's fairways, it was just another lesson in the remarkable schooling of the sixteen-year-old phenom Matteo Manassero. Playing alongside the man who had children much older than him, Manassero quietly watched and learned.

"His patience on the golf course was the main thing that struck me," said the Italian who had qualified for the Open by becoming the youngest winner of the British Amateur just a few months before.

"How calm he was even after bad shots. I learned a lot from him, but it was the patience that really hit home."

As impressed as Oxman was with his own man's round, he was just as blown away by the youngster's.

"He and his coach, who caddied for him, were very mature and deliberate about thinking through what they had to do," says Oxman. "It wasn't like . . . well, he just didn't do anything dumb. He was managing his game the same way we were managing ours.

"He's way, way beyond sixteen."

One young man beyond his age, and one older man far from it. But that first round in general was a remarkable mixture of generations.

Watson would have had the first-round lead at day's end

had not the barrel-chested, ponytailed forty-five-year-old Spaniard Miguel Ángel Jiménez closed out the evening with a 64, the veteran's best start ever in a major championship.

He was asked later if he felt guilty about knocking Watson from the top of the leaderboard. He puffed twice on his celebratory cigar and laughed.

"No, no, he's going to be a legend forever. Tom Watson is one of the guys you still have to look at, keep looking for."

The crowds agreed wholeheartedly. At every tee and every green throughout the day, Watson had been greeted with warm, familial applause from the large galleries. Though he was one of forty-four Americans in the field, twice as many as England in second place, Watson might as well have been one of the seven men from Scotland, a "homeboy" of great repute.

"I get such a warm reception," he said. "My wife and I went to a restaurant earlier this week and were recognized. It's very nice. Golf is such a strong thread running through the lives of so many Scots, even those who don't play. Everyone at least knows someone who *does* play, so they understand the passion in the game. Of course, I think my winning five Opens helps, too.

"I also like what I see and hear from the children in Scotland. They are still very civilized. I love them because they are polite and they ask you for things in the right way. They still have good manners. I like to be called 'Mr. Watson.' It shows respect. I give that same respect to my elders. I was brought up that way."

If it could not be one of theirs in blood, it might as well be one of theirs in heart. Chances of the former appeared once again slim.

Scotland's last Open champion was Paul Lawrie in 1999 at Carnoustie, and he would not have even sniffed the play-off that rainy Sunday evening had the Frenchman Jean Van de Velde not commited one of the greatest gaffes in Open history on the 18th hole of regulation. He needed only a double bogey at the par-4 finishing hole but wound up tripling the hole and sending things into a dark-threatened playoff with American Justin Leonard and Lawrie. The latter's comeback from 10 shots behind at the start of Sunday's play may be an Open record that stands forever.

Still, the meager showing of Scottish players at Turnberry continued to be a thorn in that country's golfing side. For a land that takes righteous pride in being the birthplace of golf (though parts of Europe might argue with that), Scotland's production of contending professionals continues to flounder. Its only contribution, in fact, to the 138th Open was the Colin Montgomerie Links Golf Academy, which is attached to the clubhouse and golf grounds. Montgomerie, who was one of the seven Scots in the opening field but who did not make the weekend cut, remained the country's dying hope for a return to the game's upper tier despite being forty-five years old when he teed it up that Thursday.

Only two Scots—Lawrie and David Drysdale—made the cut. More men from South America made the weekend.

In all, fifty players broke par on the opening day, unheard

of even in the most benign of Open conditions. And Watson, though the oldest by far, was not the only member of AARP to play well. Fifty-two-year-old Mark O'Meara and forty-nine-year-old Mark Calcavecchia, both former Open champions, began with 67s.

Many in the field, of course, took abrupt notice of Watson's name near the top of the leaderboard.

"I think if he plays the way he played today," said Steve Stricker, who finished the day a shot behind him, "he can beat Tiger Woods and anyone else."

"Amazing," said the 1999 Open champion Lawrie. "The golf ball has no idea how old you are."

Beating Woods, the number-one player in the world and far and away the heavy betting favorite, would not be an issue. The temperamental star opened with a club-tossing 71, missing some targets off the tee by as many as 40 yards, and stood 7 shots off the lead, his largest first-round deficit ever at the Open. While Watson worked the wind like a maestro, Woods never seemed comfortable as it changed seemingly by the moment.

While a great majority of the fans were spending their time watching the Woods implosion, Watson still had more than his share of beholders and he basked in their welcome.

Watson, like Nicklaus, detested the idea of becoming a ceremonial golfer, someone taking up space in the field, there simply because of past accomplishments and not present capabilities. But that said, as he made his way around the 7,211 yards, he never once turned down an opportunity to make eye contact with the supportive galleries. They would cry his name in their lyrical lilt and he would smile and wave and thank them each in his own way for the years and years of love. And so in essence on that opening day, Watson was returning their favor by giving them ceremony *and* great play.

As they were leaving the scorers' cabin, a stark white trailer marked RECORDER, Neil Oxman turned to his boss and simply said, "You know, this is a thing."

Watson smiled, totally getting it, but let it pass.

"I knew what he was talking about but I'm programmed," he says. "I always program myself. Whenever I play, I try to do my absolute best. Knowing during those four days there will be ups and downs. Part of those times, I have a feeling like I can win and I always draw on that feeling.

"It's a feeling that life is really good and I am in the place I want to be. When you aren't playing well, you aren't in that place. You need to change something or do something to get to that place. That's always been my task. When you start off with that feeling, that relieves part of the burden and pressure."

OFFICIAL SCORECARD
THE OPEN CHAMPIONSHIP 2009
TURNBERRY

Tom WATSON
Game 9
Thursday 16 July at 7:58 am

FOR R&A USE ONLY 9.2

ROUND 1

18 HOLE TOTAL

65

THIS ROUND 65

VERIFIED

ROUND 1

Hole	1	2	3	4	5	6	7	8	9	Out
Yards	354	428	489	166	474	231	538	454	449	3583
Par	4	4	4	3	4	3	5	4	4	35
Score	3	4	3	3	4	3	5	4	4	33

Hole	10	11	12	13	14	15	16	17	18	In	Total
Yards	456	175	451	410	448	206	455	559	461	3621	7204
Par	4	3	4	4	4	3	4	5	4	35	70
Score	3	3	3	4	4	3	4	4	4	32	65

Signature of Marker

Signature of Competitor _____ Tom Watson

6

IN THE SHADOWS

As Tom Watson was capturing the first-round hysteria, Stewart Cink sat in a stiff, uncomfortable chair in a small room across from a nurse. The medical trailer near the Turnberry clubhouse was cramped and held just two stations. Cink had to duck to enter the door.

The tall, bald American's mind raced through a haze of sickening fright. His neck was stiff and sore, and his joints ached with a fury usually reserved for ten-hour practice days. He had read in the local newspaper just that morning about the continuing worldwide swine flu epidemic. Swine flu, or H1N1, had begun its rampage in Mexico early in the year, and by the time the world turned its eyes toward Turnberry in July, hundreds had died and many thousands more had been infected. It was being called a global pandemic, touching every corner of the earth, offering up the exact same symptoms Cink was experiencing.

"It said Great Britain was predicting millions would get

it and half that many would die," the thirty-six-year-old re-calls with a shudder. "I immediately thought, 'Well, do we test for swine flu here?' But the nurse said they weren't that worried about it. I didn't quite understand that, but I think I was too sick to pursue it.

"Easy for her to say."

Strangely enough, just minutes before, he had very qui-etly shot an opening 4-under-par 66 and stood, at that point, only a shot off Watson's headline-stealing lead. He had posted six birdies and two bogeys and played with the effort-less flow of a man in a comfortable zone. Looks deceived.

Both the sickness and the shadow would remain for the rest of the tournament. Cink, a veteran with five wins on the PGA Tour, would be like a rowboat in a tsunami, safe but lost in the furor.

"The adrenaline worked very much in my favor," he re-members. "I was so sick, but it took away the symptoms. It's sorta like grease on a wheel, it makes everything smoother. When you're feeling poor, be it an injury or just illness, adrenaline will get you through.

"It was a tough week for me. Not a great place to play when you're sick like I was. Cold and windy, I had more clothes on than usual. And because my normal routine is to play, hit balls, putt, go through my drills, and then go to the gym, well, I never did any of that except for warming up.

"I never did anything. I was totally off my normal rou-tine."

True to his quiet, self-effacing nature, Cink never told

anyone other than his wife and the nurse that he was sick. But as his road to late Sunday afternoon and a date with destiny now took on a more somber tone, his journey *to* Turnberry itself had its own twists.

Born and raised in Alabama, Cink accepted a golf scholarship to Georgia Tech and played alongside future fellow touring pro and Open champion David Duval there. While his golf was beginning to take championship form, his private life was following suit. He married his wife, Lisa, during his junior year and they had their first son, Connor, while still in college. Life was good and it was also much more grounded than that of most of his teammates.

He turned professional in 1995, finished tied for eighteenth in his first event, and then joined the minor-league Nationwide Tour and startled the world. He won three times, including the tour championship, set records for money earned, and bolted to the PGA Tour the following season.

So far, so good. So very good.

He won a tournament his rookie year, finished the season twenty-ninth in earnings, and became the first man to be named Nationwide Player of the Year and, next year, PGA Tour Rookie of the Year.

He didn't win again for another two seasons and perhaps, before Turnberry, was best known to the general public for missing a very short putt for bogey in the 2001 U.S. Open. A bogey would have put him in the playoff with Mark Brooks and Retief Goosen. Instead, the double bogey sent him into a putting wasteland for the next few years.

"It was anxiety," he says now. "I didn't like anxiety over missing."

Fast-forward just two months prior to the Open to May 2009 and the Players Championship, considered the fifth major by most players.

"I wasn't playing well," he says. "I wasn't happy. I wasn't getting any satisfaction in my rounds. In my life, I have other sources of real satisfaction and being Christian gives me a huge cornerstone deeply rooted so that when I make big changes, they are superficial.

"But poor play made me say I have to take stock in what I'm doing. I missed the cut at the Players and, long story short, decided to go to work with Mo Pickens, who is a sports psychologist. That was the kicking day. I was so uncomfortable with the way I was playing, just not pleased with myself for letting this go on, and finally I put my foot down.

"I had been working with another guy, Preston Waddington, who wasn't really a sports psychologist. He is everything a sports psychologist is not—at least that's what his claim is. He was great. He taught me a lot about myself. I'd known him for about nine years and he taught me a lot about how the mind works on the golf course. How self-esteem plays a part in golf and how to suppress your fears out there. I got a lot out of it. But I just think I ran my course with him so I decided to make a big change."

He paused, deep in thought.

"That and changing back to the short putter. I had used a long putter for about six years but I needed to change. I felt like the only way for the change to take hold was to completely switch everything. I felt like if I let go of the belly putter, I would sync back into the old form."

Dr. Morris Pickens became part of the extended Cink family, having worked with Cink's good friends Zach Johnson and Lucas Glover as they won the 2008 Masters and 2009 U.S. Open, respectively. Though professional golf is a very individual game, it is often played by a team of men and women. Today's frontline golfer comes with a posse of sorts, from his caddie to his swing coach, to his psychologist and his trainer. Frank Williams, Butch Harmon, Mo Pickens, and Chris Nosh in Cink's case. And don't forget the spouse, who weighs in often, and there seem to be few more in tune with her husband and his game than Lisa Cink. But next to her, the psychologist works the deepest.

"We knew each other on a personal basis, obviously," says Cink, "but when I started working with him on a professional basis, we really clicked and I really understood his theories.

"With Mo, it was a complete overhaul of my routine and my functions. It gave me something to rely on under pressure. To focus away from the results, which is what I had been doing. I was hitting poorly, putting poorly. All along, if you look at my stats and results, I was playing well, making cuts, finishing in the top ten, but that's not what I was playing for, just making the cut. I wanted to be in contention and to be a factor.

"I felt like I was falling into irrelevancy and I didn't

want to be irrelevant. So I figured the only way was to go back to the short putter and completely overhaul my pre-shot routine. Give myself a focus, a purpose, something to strive for."

Pickens, who sold pharmaceuticals before becoming Zen master to the majors, had watched Cink from a short distance for several years.

"He didn't have a routine and didn't practice productively," he says. "Physically, visually, mentally, he was all over the board. He was pretty lost."

"Subconsciously," says Cink, "you can only focus on one thing at a time. If you're over your shot and thinking about your putting, there's no chance but to guide the ball. And in the game of golf, you aren't gonna be successful doing that. If you just let it go, your body and mind are going to work together and produce a good shot. Sorta like a three-point shooter in basketball or a fastball pitcher. You can't guide. If you operate under the premise that the mind can only think of one thing at a time, then if you focus on what you're doing in your preshot routine and trust it, your mind will be freed up. It all leads to nice shots."

Immediately in the weeks preceding the Open, Cink began to see results.

"My putting stats right away jumped sky-high when I started working with Mo," he says. "I just felt a lot of confidence and started introducing him to the rest of my game, although it's tough on me and my mind. That was the biggest change on my preshot routine, that and getting rid of the long putter."

And so, armed with a new psychologist, a new putter, and a new attitude, Stewart Cink packed his family and headed east from their home in Atlanta to the magic kingdom. They would spend a week in Ireland before making the short hop to Scotland and the Open.

Or not.

"I had planned the whole trip." He laughs. "I love doing that, dotting all the i's and crossing the t's. But we get to the Atlanta airport and I forgot that kids' passports expire in five years. And the boys' had. I didn't even check. So obviously, we didn't make that flight."

They rerouted to Washington, D.C., took advantage of a connection at the passport agency, and rearranged their itinerary. They finally flew into Dublin and promptly drove across the country.

"It was trains, planes, and automobiles," he told me, "but we enjoyed it. Didn't stop us from playing eighteen holes that night. My youngest son, Reagan, played eighteen holes just to say he played. We had a great time, the wind blew hard, nobody played well. It was like a hurricane.

"I wanted the week in Ireland to show the kids links golf. I wanted them to see the difference between playing at home and playing at, say, Ballybunion. Totally different game.

"Frankly, we were having such a great time in Ireland,

we didn't go into Turnberry until Tuesday of tournament week. We were gonna go on Monday, but because we were enjoying ourselves so much, we just said let's wait.

"Listen, I was at peace with myself. I had no expectations. I didn't go over to the British Open set on wrestling the Claret Jug out of anyone's hands and bringing it back to Duluth, Georgia."

Though beginning to feel the first stages of his mysterious sickness, he finally settled in for his eleventh attempt at the Open where his record was a poor one, despite an avowed devotion. He had one top ten prior to Turnberry and had missed three of the previous four cuts.

"I love links golf," he says. "I think loving it doesn't always translate into scores. I understood that quickly. It really is the best way to play golf. It's the most testing. To me, the winner of the British Open is the one who played the best. You just have to hit all the shots. You can't hide any weaknesses. It exposes everything. There are different ways the course can present itself on any given day with wind, rough, all that."

He played a practice round by himself on that Tuesday, meeting up with his swing coach, Butch Harmon, and then playing the first six holes before finishing up on eighteen.

"Man, I had no expectations. I could have shot two 80s and still been happy.

"Funny, I played my only full practice round on Wednesday with Zach [Johnson] and Lucas [Glover]. I don't remember playing great, but I do recall walking over to the driving range and running into [ABC announcer Mike] Tirico. He and I were the only ones out there. He asked how it was going, whether I had what it takes to win. I said I didn't have a lot.

"I was just having a good time. I had no expectations. I didn't mean that in a negative way. I am happy either way. Looking forward to playing, that's it.

"I said I had nothing, it's how I felt. I wasn't assessing myself. I had no idea where my current game would put me in the tournament. Where did I deserve to finish—tenth, first, what? It all goes back to that peaceful feeling I was having with my kids, my wife, everyone was having a good time, getting along—which is kinda rare. And there was the sick thing."

But as so often happens in golf, whether at the professional level or with a 20-handicapper, there comes an "Aha!" moment. It happened for Stewart Cink on the range that very afternoon.

"I don't know if it was divine intervention or what, but I started hitting the ball solidly. I found something really good. I felt like I abbreviated my shoulder turn a little bit, got my left shoulder back over my right knee, and I found I was able to control my shots right to left.

"I was like, hey, I'm going with this. I didn't tell my caddie or Butch or anyone. I just came up with it on my own. I went to the course with it on Thursday."

But along with the aha came the oh no. A mixed bag of emotions. Something good was happening with his swing while something very bad was happening with his body.

"I played really well that first round," he says, "despite the aches and cold sweat. Sixty-six will do that."

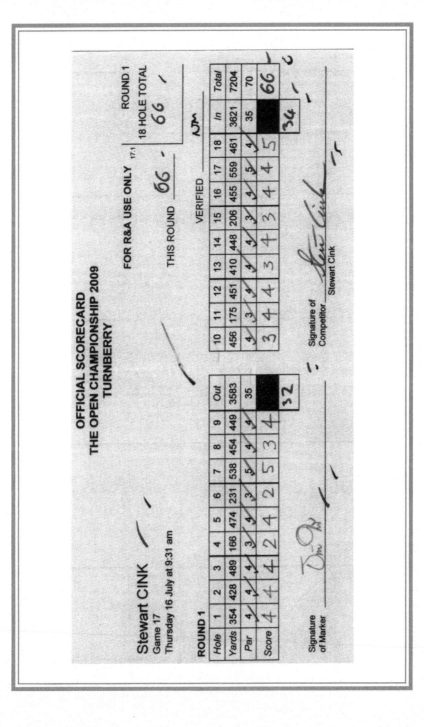

OFFICIAL SCORECARD
THE OPEN CHAMPIONSHIP 2009
TURNBERRY

Stewart CINK
Game 17
Thursday 16 July at 9:31 am

FOR R&A USE ONLY   ROUND 1
18 HOLE TOTAL

THIS ROUND 66

66

VERIFIED

ROUND 1

Hole	1	2	3	4	5	6	7	8	9	Out
Yards	354	428	489	166	474	231	538	454	449	3583
Par	4	4	4	3	4	3	5	4	4	35
Score	4	4	4	2	4	2	5	3	4	32

Hole	10	11	12	13	14	15	16	17	18	In	Total
Yards	456	175	451	410	448	206	455	559	461	3621	7204
Par	4	3	4	4	4	3	4	5	4	35	70
Score	3	4	4	3	4	3	4	4	5	34	66

Signature
of Marker

Signature of
Competitor

Stewart Cink

7

TURNBERRY TAKES FLIGHT

The Open Championship is a presumptuous event if only in name. There are, after all, nearly fifty such national golf championships around the planet, from the Mauritius Open to the Slovenia and Uruguay Opens. But because the British version was presumably the first, played over a twelve-hole collection of humps and bumps known as Prestwick Golf Club in Scotland for the first time in 1860, it is allowed the right to simply be called *the* Open.

One would think, considering all the egos involved, that the American version would usurp that glory, but every summer, the *United States* Open is held in June, finishing up on Father's Day, and *the* Open Championship comes almost precisely one month later.

In the century and a half since that modest debut at Prestwick, there have been fourteen venues for the Open, from Royal Cinque Ports, Prince's, and Royal St George's all bunched together near the white cliffs of Dover in the south-eastern corner of England, to Carnoustie in the east of Scotland and Turnberry in the west. For a moment in time, they took the Open to Northern Ireland and the wondrously difficult Royal Portrush. Never again, quietly shouted the fathers, it must remain for the rest of time within the contiguous borders of the island that is Great Britain.

The current rotation, set by the Royal and Ancient Golf Club of St Andrews, which is the governing body, includes only nine courses. Each must be a links layout, in touch with the sea at some point, laid out accepting what the land offers. While most golf courses require earth being moved to form hills and valleys, links courses generally follow the natural flow of the land. There are no trees, simply stark and unforgiving land that seems to roll forever, speckled with gorse and heather and long wispy fescue just waiting to gobble up a Titleist at any time.

Five of the Open courses are located in Scotland, the other four in England. Five of the nine—Hoylake, Birkdale, Lytham & St Annes, St George's, and Troon—are designated as royals. There seems to be little rhyme or reason behind that entitlement. A senior member of the British royal family, from king or queen to duke, visits a club, enjoys the experience, and bestows the royal designation. That is followed by a period of membership as patron or merely a brief association as visitor or guest.

"There's no such thing as application," one member of

a royal club cheekily proclaimed. "And you have to be careful how you treat his or her highness. There've been a few incidents of the title being withdrawn, so we are always very careful to be very polite to our benefactor whenever he is here."

At last count, there were sixty-two such "royal" clubs around the world, from Royal Nairobi in Kenya to Royal Marianske Lazne in the Czech Republic. Only six have received the prefix since World War II, but two of those—Royal Troon and Royal Birkdale—are on the Open rota. Thirty reside in Great Britain. Six are in North America—but all north of the United States border. (One suspects the royals have a long memory and thus feel they have given enough to the upstart Americans over the centuries.)

The Royal and Ancient Golf Club of St Andrews in Scotland was the first, in 1834.

Oddly, perhaps like *the* Open itself, the Old Course at St Andrews is never referred to as Royal St Andrews, chiefly because the club is totally separate from the actual golf course itself. (Pay close attention, this can become a bit confusing.) The R&A is a private club while the course is so open to the public that one often has to wait for townspeople walking their dogs across the fairways before hitting shots.

While Prestwick held the first twelve Opens and twenty-four in all before falling off the rotation in 1925 due to lack of space, and while St Andrews has been a regular since 1873, the forefathers didn't turn to Turnberry until 1977.

Turnberry is a magnificent resort, unlike the other more private clubs, and is the youngest on the current list, but it
wasn't ignored because it didn't pay its dues.

The ravages of war left direct pockmarks on a great
many of England and Scotland's classic golf courses in the
twentieth century, but few took quite the hit that Turnberry
did. For the last few years of World War I, Turnberry was
transformed into a flying school to train pilots in aerial gun-
nery. In fact, all the lockers were cleaned out in the clubhouse and used to store machine guns.

Turnberry once again was transformed from a golfing
paradise into a military airfield for World War II. Fairways
became four-foot-thick concrete runways to accommodate
the much heavier aircraft that had evolved since World War
I. Even today, you can see the faint outline of long-abandoned
strips, the only reminders of Turnberry's great sacrifice with
the exception of the noble memorial that overlooks the 12th
green, honoring those who lost their lives in the training.

One name on that memorial that is perhaps the most
ironic in all of war waging: Lt. Reginald Milburn Makepeace.

No, Turnberry's service to Mother Britain would never
be questioned. But its availability to the large crowds that
attend Opens was. Turnberry was built in 1906 as an alterna-
tive on the west coast to golfing retreats like Balmoral in
Edinburgh and Gleneagles in Perthshire. Built by the Glasgow
and South Western Railway, it attracted large numbers of
holiday golfers. Tourists could board a northbound train in

the heat of a London evening and be ready for a chilly wind-blown round of golf at Turnberry the next morning. The actual structure was called the Station Hotel for the first half of its century-long existence.

That lasted until the 1940s, when the railway that went directly to the front door of the picturesque hotel stopped running. The hotel had been turned into a wartime hospital and there seemed no need for the railway, so it was not only retired but the rails actually ripped up. Since then, the only way to reach Turnberry is along a pair of narrow two-lane roads that border the property, one through picturesque farmland and the small town of Maybole, the other called "the coast road," which winds along the shoreline on its way to and from the small town of Ayr.

As a holiday destination, it has always seemed perfect, a hidden gem tucked away 'tween the hills and the sea. It *should* be difficult to reach, then, and more difficult to escape. But as an Open venue, with the event's inherent entourage of giant tents and citylike television compounds and a daily attendance in the tens of thousands, it seemed to make little sense.

Still, in 1977, the R&A took a gamble and brought the Open along those back roads, and the glorious and dramatic tableau that followed paid off handsomely. There, this same Tom Watson and an older Jack Nicklaus did the kind of battle that became known as the best Open championship in its long history, the famous Duel in the Sun.

Watson, just twenty-seven at the time, and Nicklaus, ten

years his elder, separated themselves from a sterling field that weekend to the point where third-place finisher Hubert Green famously said, "Hey, I won my championship. I don't know what those other two guys were playing." Green finished 11 shots behind them.

Back and forth they went like two heavyweight fighters, trading blows, captivating the enormous galleries, many of whom were in various stages of undress thanks to a most uncommon and baking sun. The two combatants had gone head-to-head in the past. In fact, Watson had taken the Masters from Nicklaus just three months earlier. They were rivals in those days, not the great friends they would become in the years ahead. Of Watson's eight career major titles, Nicklaus finished second in four of them and was third and fourth in two more.

Still, tied with three holes to go on the final day at Turnberry, they stood on the 16th tee and soaked it all in.

"This is as good as it gets, eh?" Watson said to Nicklaus as they looked out upon the sea of sunburned Scots.

Nicklaus grinned back. "You bet it is."

An hour later, after a short birdie putt on the 18th, Watson had his second Open Championship. The modest Claret Jug, first given in 1873, would become an important part of Watson's trophy case over the decades, but this one was perhaps the most special. Watson would return to Turnberry in 2003 for the Senior British Open and win in a playoff, just four days after he and Nicklaus had ceremoniously dedicated a plaque there. It is common for clubs to give names to each of their holes. The 18th at Ailsa would forever be known as Duel in the Sun.

He barely stopped to notice the words etched on a granite pillar at the 18th tee in 2009, letting his memories of that remarkable day be his guide.

8

WHY NOT?

After signing his first-round scorecard and having a word with Oxman, Tom Watson stepped into my world in another trailer directly across from the recorders' cabin. It was disguised as a walnut-paneled locker room, supposedly resembling the players' actual clubhouse fifty feet away. As technicians wired him for sound, he could barely keep the smile from overflowing. There was a bubble that refused to be burst.

"The body is a little older, but the enthusiasm out there was very similar," he told me in his distinctive Midwestern clip. "It was a wonderful day to play. Little wind, the course was obviously defenseless. All the scores under par, a lot of them because of that. It was a good beginning round for me and the wind ought to pick up tomorrow. She will have some teeth to her, and I look forward to that."

I touched the replica of the Claret Jug that sat between us. Talk, I asked, about this trophy.

"I've had a pretty good haul over here. I've played some

of my best golf over here. I've always enjoyed the challenge of getting the ball close to the hole in these windy conditions. The greens are firm. The fairways are firm. When you add the wind to it, the ball doesn't stop right by the hole. You have to filter it in there.

"I've [mentioned] my ability to play against the kids. I can't play against them at Augusta. It's just too soft and too long. I am hitting the wrong clubs into the holes there, but I've said a links golf course, you get the ball out there and rolling. I kept it in play today and basically missed one green at the 14th and the rest of them I was putting for par and birdies."

Three more rounds. Can you keep it up?

"Who knows? Why not?"

There can be a warmth to Tom Watson's eyes; there can also be an icy stare that makes you want to slide under the nearest chair. I have felt both over the years and the latter is a most uncomfortable confrontation. In retrospect, I suppose "Can you keep it up?" *is* a ridiculous question for a man who has won more than sixty times worldwide in his career, made over $21 million, and been inducted into the World Golf Hall of Fame. And yet here he was, in the waning moments of his fifty-ninth year, not having played in over a month, facing the best young players in the world.

Why not indeed? How silly of me. And the look in those eyes clearly said precisely that, perhaps in stronger terms.

I had seen it many times over the decades on the heels of a question of poor choice, in his mind. One of the most glaring, for me, came during the early stages of the 1996 U.S. Open at Oakland Hills in suburban Detroit. Watson was playing very well, finished tied for thirteenth, in fact, but the story for many of us in the media that week was the emergence of the young star named Tiger Woods.

Still an amateur (though *what* an amateur, with three U.S. Amateur Championships under his twenty-eight-inch belt), Woods was playing in his second U.S. Open after having withdrawn from the first a year before with a wrist injury.

Those of us with notebooks and video cameras, charged with bringing home the story of the day, were eager to get reactions from the veteran players to this remarkable youngster.

It was my misfortune to ask that of Tom Watson on the very day he himself had climbed close to the lead. I will never forget it. The eyes squinted and the smoke wisped from his ears as he demanded to know why I wanted to talk about the kid and not him.

"Ask me about my round," he said sharply. "I don't want to talk about Tiger Woods."

I waited for a smile, an "aw, I'm just joshing" moment. It never came. He had fought through a hot and humid afternoon in the wake of one of the worst thunderstorms in U.S. Open history, leaving the lengthy course a swamp. He had played well and felt he deserved a better question.

Properly chastised, I backed off and asked, er, what club he had used on 17. It was the only other question I had, and it taught me a very valuable lesson when it came to interviewing Tom Watson: Look him dead in the eye and give him his due.

If there is anything we all have learned over the decades of having the pleasure (or pain) of his company, is that he is as tough and hard-nosed and determined as anyone ever on tour. His competitors know that, his friends know that, so do his neighbors. One of the most ardent reminders of just how principled this man is came nearly twenty years ago in his hometown of Kansas City, Missouri.

————

Watson, who grew up at the Kansas City Country Club, just across the border in Kansas City, Kansas, learned his game there, became a junior member when he was twenty-one and a full-time member not long after that, abruptly and angrily resigned in 1990 when the club reportedly refused membership to Henry Bloch, the cofounder of the income-tax preparatory franchise H&R Block, because Bloch was Jewish.

"This is something I cannot live with," he told the *Kansas City Star*, "because my family is Jewish."

Watson is not, but his first wife, Linda, was.

"I felt it was a religious issue and I can't live with that. I feel more than uncomfortable. I think it's wrong. It's more than my conscience could bear."

The resignation came as Watson was at the very pinnacle of his reign as a major champion, having won the Open five times already, the U.S. Open twice, and the Masters twice. It made national headlines and a terrible firestorm in Kansas City. A principled man standing up for what he believed was right, despite the fact that he had grown up at the club, learned the game there from his father and from the head pro Stan Thirsk, who was his coach.

He quietly rejoined the club when the exclusionary clause was dropped.

There is much to this man, as there is to most. In the space of six weeks in 1998, he quit drinking alcohol cold turkey and faced a bitter divorce from the woman he had dated first in high school and married shortly after graduating from Stanford University. Though he remains very private regarding the divorce, he talked publicly of the drink, hoping it would make a difference with others.

"I stopped all by myself," he said. "Drinking is a choice. It's a social issue, a peer-pressure issue. If I had faced trouble giving it up, I would have gotten some help. But I managed."

It apparently had nothing to do with the divorce from Linda, who had become known, unfairly, simply as "Mrs. Tom Watson" for twenty-five years.

"She is smart, beautiful, energetic, fiery, loyal," he was quoted as saying. "People will always be attracted to her. But she is going to have to define herself in a new way."

And so Thomas Sturges Watson is a man who fought demons, both his and others, and in his own quiet, thoughtful, absolute way, he has won more than he has lost.

A golf tournament, you see, is easy in comparison. Why not indeed?

9

THE BAG MAN

They stand in the middle of the fairway nearly as one. The player in argyle and gray, the caddie in standard white bib, wire-rimmed glasses, and tan shorts. It is midway through the first round and they are deep in conversation. The wind whistles softly off the Irish Sea to their left.

Surely they are making their club selection or perhaps choosing a spot in the distance as an aiming target. Perhaps they are even having a casual laugh over the poor Scotsman asleep in a nearby thicket.

It is more likely, however, that Tom Watson and Neil Oxman are talking American politics: health-care reform, a recent Drudge Report, the state of the nation under its new president.

"Thursday and Friday at the Open, we play threesomes," says Oxman, "so there is more time to chat. We talk a lotta politics, healthy discussions."

He laughs.

"We need to get our talking in during the first two

rounds, 'cause on Saturday and Sunday when we're only two-somes, it's hectic. We don't have that luxury. You have no time. It's get the yardage, hit the shot, fill the divot, get the yardage, hit the shot, on and on."

The relationship between the average player and his caddie can be a curious, unsettling one. Some last for years, others for eighteen holes or less. The men in bibs can be simply carriers, sometimes called loopers, or they can be anything from a close friend to a shrink. When it comes to golf, however, they advise and consent but then shut up. Bottom line: It is the man with the club who has the final say.

For much of Tom Watson's magical career, a lanky smiling young man named Bruce Edwards was his caddie, best friend, confidant, everything good that a bag man can be. Their relationship began, improbably, in the summer of 1973. Teenagers Edwards and Oxman were good friends, but while Oxman at that time had a steady bag on tour already, Edwards was on the outside, waiting, wondering if he had chosen the right career. Oxman introduced him to twenty-four-year-old Watson at the Greater St. Louis Golf Classic.

"I saw this long-haired kid in jeans asking me to caddy," Watson told John Feinstein in his wonderful book *Caddie for Life*. "He was polite, I remember that. So I said, 'Okay, we'll try it for a week and see what happens.'"

Edwards hesitantly carried the young pro's bag that week and never left it again, even thirty years later when he was in the final stages of the devastating amyotrophic lateral sclerosis, Lou Gehrig's disease. His death took Watson's soul and twisted it, for this hadn't been simply someone who had carried Tom's golf bag, handing him clubs and finding him yardage. They had grown as one during their partnership. In the midst of thirty-five PGA victories and five times as many defeats together, they became brothers, best friends.

Early on a Thursday morning in April of 2004, as Watson was preparing for his opening round at the Masters, he got the phone call from Edwards's wife, Marsha, that he had been dreading.

"Hilary and I just looked at each other," Watson said later that day to the gathered media, "and said, how typical that he died on the opening day of the Masters, his favorite tournament."

How Watson managed those lonely eighteen holes that sunny day, only he knows. He wandered as if in a daze, tears lingering at the edge of his eyes, waiting to be unleashed. The 76 that he somehow carved out of the wondrous old Augusta National layout was nearly an afterthought. In his right rear pocket was Edwards's old Augusta National yardage book.

"With it there," said Watson later, "I felt like he was with me. Of course, I knew he was, anyway."

"Bruce didn't want to just sit on the couch and watch the Masters," Watson's wife told him, "he wanted to sit on your shoulder."

In his postround press conference that Thursday, Watson

put words to angry emotions that had been building within him for a year. His eyes, flooded and red, blazed. He had a bully pulpit and was determined to use it.

"First of all," he said, "I just want to say damn this disease! Damn it! They are going to find a cure. We don't have one right now.

"There's a lot of research going on right now. It's not for naught. There is good stuff going. Let's suffice it to say we don't have one [a cure] yet but we will get there. We are going to get there."

Watson was devastated by the loss but quickly turned it as positive as he could by becoming involved with a foundation called Driving 4 Life, to raise money to fight ALS. In 2004 alone, the year of Edwards's death, it raised more than $3 million, a third of which came directly out of Watson's pocket. By the end of 2009, they had raised $9 million with over 250 national fund-raising events, many of which Watson is directly involved with.

It is how Watson goes about his life. It also speaks to the generous professional golf community.

———

One of the final times Bruce Edwards caddied for his old friend was in the 2003 U.S. Open at Olympia Fields outside Chicago, just months after being diagnosed. At every green along the way in the opening round, he and Watson were greeted with an outpouring of love and respect that constantly reduced the pair to tears.

Word had spread quickly and the galleries thundered their prayers, as if they felt they could cure the man with their love. Through the salty film, Watson brought the years roaring back with a startling 65, similar in many ways to the 65 with which he began the 2009 Open Championship.

They came tumbling back to earth in the final three rounds, however, finishing a dozen shots behind winner Jim Furyk, but their point had been made and the world was aware. Ten months later, in the hours leading up to the Masters, Bruce Edwards died.

Neil Oxman, who had paired them thirty-one years previous, stepped in to take Watson's bag, and though the golfer was an elderly fifty-four and Oxman just four years his junior, they instantly clicked. It was surprising in many ways but primarily in the undertone of their fairway debates.

Watson, once a liberal, is now what Oxman calls "an old-fashioned, WASPy Heinz-Rockefeller Republican." Oxman is a longtime ardent Democrat whose Philadelphia firm, the Campaign Group, manages political campaigns. Because Watson seldom plays more than a dozen tournaments a year, Oxman has the time to devote to what he clearly calls his "second career."

And to further mystify an already curious relationship, Watson and Oxman work together for the most part only in odd years when there are no political campaigns to run. Oxman makes an exception for the Open Championship and the Senior British Open, which immediately follows. So Oxman worked 2003, gave the bag over to Edwards's longtime friend and veteran caddie Jeff Burrell in 2004, and when Burrell died of cancer, another veteran, Todd Newcomb, became Watson's looper while Oxman was on the trail for ballots, not birdies.

"I've managed over 650 campaigns over the years," he says, "and caddied in more than 400 tournaments. I am a caddie first and a political consultant when I have time."

The Campaign Group, which he cofounded, has offices in La Jolla as well as Philadelphia, and has represented well over a hundred candidates since 2002, three-quarters of whom have won their races. Among the more high-profile candidates have been Pennsylvania governor Ed Rendell, New Mexico governor Bill Richardson, Delaware senator Tom Carper, Governor Jay Nixon of Missouri, and Philadelphia mayor Michael Nutter.

Aside from carrying for one of the greatest golfers in history and managing big-time political campaigns, Oxman also finds time to see as many as 230 movies a year, reviewing them for NPR and other outlets.

And so as they stand side by side in the middle of the Scottish fairway, waiting for the game to evolve, one can only imagine the discussion. Is it the cost of war this time or *The Taking of Pelham 123*? Is it Obama or O'Toole?

Or is it simply, "176 to the front, 181 to the flag, wind out of the west helping a bit. You hit 7 here in yesterday"?

10

THE SECOND ROUND: NO-BRAINERS

Your job, guys, is to write the story and my job is to make the story.

—Tom Watson, July 18, 2009

It was Friday and, just as almost everyone expected, the wheels were coming off. While Thursday's first round was as pure as it gets, the second began with a torrent of bogeys. And why not? The man was six weeks shy of sixty! This surely would be like that painful U.S. Open in 2003 when the emotional toll became too hard to handle.

There was no way Tom Watson could maintain Thursday's good fortune. Especially now that, as he himself put it, "Lady Turnberry had the silk gloves off and was fighting back." Though the sun remained strong, the wind howled as if it barreled off a ski slope on Ireland's east coast and came roaring across the sea unimpeded.

It was what old-timers in these parts call a "real wind," and it took its toll early and often, especially on Watson.

Wearing a tan sweater over a navy shirt with brown pin-striped slacks and the same black golf shoes, Watson tugged the familiar black cap a bit snugger over his dark red hair and peered down the first fairway. It was 1:09 and that wind was not the prevailing direction, instead coming from the north and west, at his back.

With the honor, he chose a 5-iron instead of the 4 that he had used on Thursday and let the ball ride the gale to the point where he had only 120 yards left on the 354-yard hole to the front of the green. A pitching wedge slid some 30 feet past the hole, but as he had the day before, he rolled in the putt for birdie and found himself at 6 under par for the championship.

Because of the time of the day and the noise surrounding Watson's reemergence, the gallery was much larger than during the opening round. As Neil Oxman said later, "There was stuff going on out there."

Making the turn to the 2nd hole, which parallels the first, the wind rocked Watson on his toes and he didn't handle it well. He chose the driver instead of the hybrid of day one and found the deep hay on the left. He had only 155 yards to the front of the green but could only hack it back to the fairway with a sand wedge, leaving himself just over 100 yards to the green. The wind seemed to grow with every minute. The gallery huddled in various forms of woolen protection, peering out at their hero.

Though he now had only 112 yards to the pin, he hit a full 9-iron and wound up 20 feet short of the hole, and he 2-putted from there for bogey, his first of the championship. The drive had cost him.

The 3rd hole was back downwind and for the second day in a row, Watson hit a driver and had 140 yards to the front. His 9-iron second shot left him hole high but 25 feet away, and he 2-putted for par.

It was an exercise in patience, the ultimate key to playing an Open since the very beginning. First, the wind was at his back and then into his face, back and forth, and seemingly nobody knew how to handle conditions like that quite like the old Kansan. But once again, into the wind at the par-3 4th hole, his 5-iron shot found the only bunker protecting the green, short in the face of the hill going up to the elevated green. He could not get up and down, made bogey, and suddenly was 1-over par for his round and back to 5-under for the championship. Another drive had cost him.

On most days at Turnberry, the stretch of holes between 4 and 11 are a welcome relief, for the prevailing wind is at your back. But it was precisely the opposite on this day.

The difference was measurable. On the par-4 5th hole, Watson had 194 yards left to the front of the green for his second shot where he had had only 163 the previous day. His drive was 31 yards shorter. The wind had blossomed to the point that Watson's 3-wood carried to the back fringe. Once more, he was unable to save par and carded his third bogey in the first five holes.

The par-3 6th hole was 210 yards to the front and another 22 yards to the flag. Watson hit 3-wood again, this time into one of the bunkers on the left. He could not get up and down for par, and another bogey left him just 2 under par for the championship.

He hit driver on the 7th and was left with 211 yards to the front of the green. His 5-iron rolled down off the mounding into the right rough, forcing him to chip out sideways. His wedge from 59 yards was 4 paces short of the hole, but he missed another par and now had bogeyed five of his first seven holes.

Surely, the same heads that had perked up like excited deer in an open field on Thursday, from the media center to the vast galleries across the course, simply nodded in assumed presumption on Friday. This was what sixty does to a man. Give him a calm, benign day here and he can still play. Give him a gale and we see what happens. Oh well, they thought, nice story while it lasted.

"We're on the 8th tee," recalls Neil Oxman, "and he's bogeyed four straight, and Sergio [Garcia] takes him aside and good-naturedly says, 'C'mon, old man, you can do this!' It was a wonderful moment, one I don't believe I'd ever seen before. Whether it was that or just Tom being Tom, he birdied 9 and got right back into it."

"That was a nice thing for Sergio to say. I was driving

the ball well," recalled Watson, "and I was putting myself in position to make birdies. And then it happened at 9. I turned it around there."

After parring the 8th with a driver and 2-hybrid, he came to the closing hole of the outbound nine needing to find some of that old-time magic. Ignoring the lighthouse and the castle ruins this time, blinders on and focus back, Watson drove the ball into the light rough on the right for the second straight day, leaving himself 129 yards to the front of the green. The flag was another 19 yards on, dangerously near the left side, and Watson's pitching wedge rolled to within 20 feet. He made the birdie and allowed himself a brief smile, raising both hands in supplication.

His numbers outbound that Friday were not promising: two birdies, two pars, five bogeys; five fairways hit and only four greens. But he was back to 3-under par for the Open and showing the resiliency playfully demanded by Garcia.

The gallery, which had never abandoned their "Auld Toom," reacted to the birdie with a wondrous noise that seemed to reverberate throughout the property. For some reason, the magic was returning or, perhaps more likely, it had never left but simply taken a rest.

On the 457-yard 10th hole, still into the strong wind, he hit a 3-wood, and as he and Oxman settled over the results in the middle of the fairway, a slight rain began to pelt sideways. For the first time in the championship—and the only time, as it would turn out—Oxman took out the umbrella and handed it to Watson. Both men put on rain pants and Oxman tugged the rain cover up over the clubs to keep them dry.

Watson had 155 yards to the front and another 27 to the pin. As they approached the green, the rain stopped and both men removed their rain suits and put the umbrella away. Though it rained at other times during the championship, particularly on Sunday morning, it never once dropped on Watson again, dousing him literally for one half hole in his twenty-four hours of collective work.

He 2-putted the 10th from 20 feet and remained at 2 under par for the championship.

At the 11th, the wind shifted and covered Watson's left shoulder on the sloping par 3. His 7-iron wound up hole high within 20 feet, and he made the putt for birdie. Now he had birdied the 9th and 11th and gone from 6 under for the championship all the way down to 1 under and now back to 3. It was a roller coaster that would have jumbled a normal man's very insides, but Watson seemed to handle it with a veteran calm.

The 12th hole was back into a wind that had died somewhat after the rain had gone through. Watson hit driver into the shadow of the war monument, and then pitching wedge from 139 yards, leaving him 15 feet. He 2-putted for par, and he seemed to have returned to a bit of the Thursday consistency, taking his birdies where he could find them but settling gratefully for par.

The tee box on the 13th is raised somewhat, and Watson took advantage of the wind at his back, hitting a 2-hybrid to within 92 yards of the front of the green. All he wanted on this slick green was to get it somewhere near, and he 2-putted for par.

Back into the wind, which was stiffening again, on 14, he hit a driver off the tee, avoiding the two new fairway bunkers, put a 5-iron from 165 yards within 15 feet, and 2-putted again for par. He remained 3-under for the championship, still very much a part of the leaderboard and back on the radar of those sniffing the ever-changing winds for story lines.

At the par-3 15th, he had 182 yards to the front and another 17 to the flag. He hit a 7-iron past the hole about 25 feet, and 2-putted for par.

Once again downwind at the dangerous par-4 16th, his 2-hybrid found the edge of the right bunker. His stance was awkward as he was left with 159 yards to the front. The flag was in the front, right where he didn't want it to be, for it begged a shot that could instead hit the giant slope and slide down into Wilson's Burn, which runs out to the Irish Sea. Easy to contribute a Titleist to Neptune there.

He hit 7-iron instead, all the way to the back of the green, a smart, safe play but one that left him nearly 70 feet from the flag.

He made the putt, the first of a pair of what he called "no-brainers," which had the gallery delirious. Watson raised his putter and as the ball rolled purely into the cup smiled at the fans. A no-brainer in golf is a ridiculously long putt that you're simply trying to cozy up to the hole and, for reasons unknown, you make. This happens when you're right with the golf gods. As Watson bowed to hide his huge grin, you felt those gods smiling, too.

At the par-5 17th, he hit a driver into a right-side bunker. He was forced to pitch out, paying the penalty demanded by Mackenzie Ross, the architect who redesigned the course after the Second World War. Watson had 171 yards to the front and another 18 to the flag, and his 8-iron brought him hole high on the left. He 2-putted for par, the only day of the four that he failed to birdie the relatively easy 17th.

As he came to the par-4 18th, the crowd was on its feet in appreciation. His 2-hybrid tee shot found the short right rough (in fact, the same club wound up almost in the same divot all four days). As he and Neil Oxman stood in that fairway just a few yards from the ball, the noise unbearable, instead of politics or movies or even distance, they talked spirits.

"I think Bruce is with us today," Watson said to his caddie.

"Oh, man, don't make me cry," said Oxman.

And they both did, tears staining sunburned cheeks, collecting in the corners of great smiles.

"It was at that moment," says Oxman, "that I gave a bit of thought to what might be, once I'd dried the tears. Hadn't had much time for that before. But it lasted only a few seconds and I was back to yardage, shot, divot, all that."

In fact, Watson had 185 yards to the false front and another 19 to the hole. His 7-iron rolled onto the right front of the green.

Five minutes later, with his second shot resting perhaps 55 feet across the large and undulating 18th green, Watson looked up at the faces in the stands and smiled again. *Why not?* he thought.

And then he drained the putt for birdie to get all the way back to even par for the round and 5 under for the championship—precisely where he had begun the day. As the Titleist rolled into the dead center of the hole, Watson kicked his right leg high and tugged his arms back, a huge smile creasing his face. The cheers could be heard throughout Turnberry's eight hundred acres. The mental part of Tom Watson's game had taken over and carried him through what could have been a disastrous stretch, and his patience was rewarded with the brilliant gift at the last.

Where Thursday had been near perfect, Friday was a wild ride for him. He hit three fewer fairways and two fewer greens, and while he made 28 putts on Thursday, he sank 31 on each of the next three days. He stayed busy all afternoon battling the freshening winds and toughening golf course. His five bogeys that Friday were all dead into the wind. But he held himself together through it all.

"It's something I do and have always done," he says about controlling his emotions. "I had to learn how to win when I got on tour. I had to learn my swing, had to learn what worked under pressure, and the only way to deal with that was to get there. I actually got there a number of times before I finally did win. It became easier after that. I got to the point where I trusted my golf swing and the experience of being under pressure."

Stewart Cink, meanwhile, slipped 2 more shots behind Watson with a second-round 72 and went into the weekend trailing the legend by 3. Cink struggled on the outward nine on Friday, double-bogeying the par-3 5th hole and getting 1 stroke back with a birdie at the 7th. He played the incoming nine at even par, with birdies at 16 and 17 to offset bogeys at 11 and 15.

Watson began the weekend at 5-under par 135, while Cink slipped to 2-under 138.

———

Watson came to my interview area that Friday afternoon with a different smile from the day before. This one was part flabbergast, part bemusement, part "what, you thought I wouldn't make that 60-footer?" Then he shook his head, sat down, and let the breath escape.

"No-brainers." He laughed. "Field goals, my father called them. Something is on my side right now. Things are happening my way. There is something about this place. . . ."

He watched the video on a small monitor in front of us of his early bogeys and then the nifty comeback and described them much as he would have in the ABC-TV booth where he was supposed to work over the weekend as a guest analyst. Both the network and Watson figured that his availability was surely a foregone conclusion. Even if he made the cut, which had seemed so improbable, he would likely play his third round early on Saturday morning and be on hand when American television came on the air. But astoundingly, there would be none of that, for he had other work to do. He was going to *be* the show.

"It was a special day," he told me. "I know I don't have many years left to play in the Open Championship, but I've had some wonderful memories and maybe I can make one more."

I picked up the Claret Jug that rested between us.

"Think this could be in your hands come Sunday afternoon?"

He gave me that stare again. Another stupid question.

"I wouldn't be here unless I thought it could."

While there had been fifty men under par on Thursday, only five would survive the wicked winds and manage to break 70 the following day. The two men at the top couldn't have been more different. Watson, with his decades of experience in links play, along with the American journeyman Steve Marino, whose rookie voyage on these kinds of waters had come just the day before. He had never once played links golf before coming to Turnberry four days prior. Both tied going to the weekend.

"Have you pinched yourself, Tom?" someone asked.

"I don't need to," he said with a half smile. "I'm awake."

A reporter from CNN asked what it felt like to sink the cross-country putts on 16 and again on 18.

Watson's eyes twinkled. "To somebody my age?" He chuckled. "Almost better than sex."

Hilary, standing nearby, threw her hands to her face in playful embarrassment.

————

Jack Nicklaus had played a round of friendly golf at his home course, the Bear's Club, in Jupiter, Florida, on Friday, and when he walked into the clubhouse afterward, the television was on. His old rival had just made the 60-footer at 16.

"Oh, my gosh," Nicklaus exclaimed, but he did not stay to watch the final two holes, preparing instead to go to a movie with Barbara.

When he and his wife returned, the world was at the door, wanting to know his thoughts.

"I'm never surprised to see him on top of any leaderboard," said the Golden Bear that afternoon, recalling the many times they had gone head-to-head over the decades. "He never ceases to amaze me. I have a lotta respect for him and his ability. Barbara and I are tickled pink with the first two rounds, and nothing would please me more than to see the old boy win."

If there was a tinge of envy, it didn't leak through. It is hard to imagine, however, anyone whose résumé includes such elegant wars not wanting to trade places, if for just a moment's return.

Others, men with whom Watson shared the headlines over the years, weren't so hesitant.

"Oh, my God," Lee Trevino told me later, "I actually got

my juices flowing. I told my wife, 'I'm excited, I'm almost seventy and I'm gonna go practice.'"

"I think he inspired me to play better," said Chip Beck, six years Watson's junior. "If I can play that good when I'm sixty, I will be very happy."

James Mason is a Champions Tour journeyman, one of those who came out of a club pro's job to give the seniors a shot.

"I think what Tom's doing gives everyone out here renewed vigor," he said. "They all say it used to be fifty-five was the cutoff, now it's sixty. You see that and go out and rededicate yourself to try and hit the ball as well as Tom does."

"Envy? Not a nice trait," said eighty-year-old Dow Finsterwald with a laugh. "Let's just say wow, wouldn't I love to be doing it, too."

OFFICIAL SCORECARD
THE OPEN CHAMPIONSHIP 2009
TURNBERRY

Tom WATSON
Game 35
Friday 17 July at 1:09 pm

	FOR R&A USE ONLY	ROUND 2
18 HOLE TOTAL	65	36 HOLE TOTAL
THIS ROUND	70	135
36 HOLE TOTAL	135	

VERIFIED _CTB_

ROUND 2

Hole	1	2	3	4	5	6	7	8	9	Out
Yards	354	428	489	166	474	231	538	454	449	3583
Par	④	4	4	3	4	3	5	4	④	35
Score	3	5	4	4	5	4	6	4	3	38

Hole	10	11	12	13	14	15	16	17	18	In	Total
Yards	456	175	451	410	448	206	455	559	461	3621	7204
Par	4	③	4	4	4	3	④	5	④	35	70
Score	4	2	4	4	4	3	3	5	3	32	70

Signature
of Marker _M. Warren_

Signature of
Competitor _Tom Watson_

Tom Watson

OFFICIAL SCORECARD
THE OPEN CHAMPIONSHIP 2009
TURNBERRY

Stewart CINK ✓
Game 43
Friday 17 July at 2:42 pm

	FOR R&A USE ONLY	43.1	ROUND 2
18 HOLE TOTAL	66 ✓		36 HOLE TOTAL
THIS ROUND	72 ✓		138 ✓
36 HOLE TOTAL	138 ✓		

VERIFIED _____ AJM

ROUND 2

Hole	1	2	3	4	5	6	7	8	9	Out
Yards	354	428	489	166	474	231	538	454	449	3583
Par	4	4	4	3	5	3	5	4	4	35
Score	4	4	4	5	5	3	4	3	5	37

Hole	10	11	12	13	14	15	16	17	18	In	Total
Yards	456	175	451	410	448	206	455	559	461	3621	7204
Par	4	3	4	4	4	3	3	5	4	35	70
Score	4	4	4	4	4	4	3	5	4	35	72

Signature
of Marker _____ Dr.O.F ✓ ✓

Signature of
Competitor _____ Stewart Cink

11

THE "OTHER" TW

Mouths gaped in pure astonishment that Friday evening, but it was difficult to discern the larger reason. That Tom Watson had somehow managed to pull himself together after nearly frittering away his hold on "special" and remained at the top of the giant yellow leaderboard was one thing; that the man who seemed truly destined to be there was, instead, headed home was another.

Tiger Woods, a presumptive favorite by not only the oddsmakers but also the fans and media as he searched for his fifteenth major championship, missed the cut. It was mind-boggling simply because it was only the second time in forty-nine major championships as a professional that the world's number-one player had gone home early. Take that a step farther and consider it was only the sixth time in 232 starts in his professional career. The golf world wobbled slightly on its axis.

It wasn't as if he was off his form coming in. He had won

his previous start at the AT&T National in marvelous fashion, hitting fairways and greens with the kind of precision that foretold great things yet to come. He had followed up previous victories that year with losses at the Masters and U.S. Open, but at least he had contended.

At Turnberry, he looked like a young man at cross-purposes, totally out of sorts and battling both himself and the elements. Even during the first round with the wind a mere flutter, he spent much of his time tossing bits of grass in the air, twisting his head this way and that, searching for answers that never came.

He shot a 1-over-par 71 on opening day when fifty players broke par, and followed that with a profanity-laced, club-throwing 74 on Friday.

"Kept making mistake after mistake," he grumbled on his way out.

Especially in one six-hole stretch on Friday when he went 7 over par.

It began at the par-4 8th and, like a runaway freight train, careered across the legendary links through the 13th, totally out of control. Bogey, bogey, double bogey with a lost ball, par, bogey, and then, from the middle of the 13th fairway, he missed the green, failed on a pitch shot that never got to the green, took 3 more strokes for another double bogey.

"You have to play clean to win majors," he said later, "and I haven't done that."

"You don't often see him playing shots like he did," said

Lee Westwood, who had played alongside Woods the first two rounds. "But everybody is entitled to a bad day every once in a while. It happens to us all.

"Just goes to show what a demanding test of golf this is."

One thing we have known about Tiger Woods all these years is that, no matter the state of his game, he never fails to grind. He might not have his A game, but he does his darnedest to make B work. And so it was at Turnberry. After the double at 13 put him outside the cut line, he could have given up and had his pilot start warming up the jet. But that has never been his style. Instead, he began firing back.

Seven-over par with three holes to play, he birdied the difficult 16th, reached the par-5 17th in 2, and made birdie there—giving him a chance to make the cut with a third birdie at 18. But he left himself 199 yards to the green and could not get it close enough to convert.

Dressed all in black, as if for a funeral, the world's best golfer shook hands with Westwood and their companion those first two days, the young Japanese star Ryo Ishikawa, and went in search of food.

"Starving," he muttered as he stopped for a brief, very terse chat with the stunned media.

I stepped from my interview trailer nearby and caught the eye of Woods's agent from IMG, Mark Steinberg. I raised my eyebrows in application and he simply pursed his lips and shook his head slowly. It was a dance we had done often over the decade as the superstar came off this course or that.

"Can I have a go at him?" I would silently ask.

On the occasion of a good round, Steinberg would either nod yes or whisper, "Two minutes, that's all."

On days such as this, few as they were, he needed only to shake his head.

Tom Watson, twenty-six years older and a legend of similar status, had no such keeper. Of course, being on top of the leaderboard instead of at the bottom makes for much more charitable offerings.

And so as one TW took his leave, the other had plans to stay to a glorious end.

1 2

STRAIGHT OUT OF "RETIREMENT"

It was the perfect arrow to fit the bow, and Turnberry had the archers loaded and ready to fire. For years, the argument has raged in contentious arenas:

Is golf a sport?

This is a game, after all, where men and women dress in bright colors and saddle oxfords and swing a stick at a stationary target. Providing that target, a white ball that measures 1.7 inches in diameter and weighs 1.6 ounces, goes semistraight, they walk casually down neatly mowed runways to find it and hit it again. No one is allowed to make noise while the ball is being struck. No one is allowed to play defense and nudge an opponent off balance. The whole endeavor can take as many as six hours to accomplish, though that is surely frowned upon. If it rains or snows too hard or if the wind blows the ball around, a siren is sounded and, on the professional level, vehicles are brought to take the players to cover and safety.

This, then, is a sport?

No one denies the physical and mental skills involved in such play. No one (certainly nobody who has actually tried the game) claims it doesn't belong among our pastimes. Just don't presume to call it a sport, some rail. Don't put it in the same ranks as football or hockey or baseball.

And so when Old Tom Watson went out in the early morning hours of July 16, 2009, and proceeded to beat nearly everyone in the field of 156 and then made it hold up for a second straight day, those valiant debaters raised the cry once again. He was like a man coming out of deep retirement for these four days.

"How can you say it's a sport when a 59-year-old man nearly wins a major," wrote Mike Freeman of CBS Sports .com. "The story may be inspirational but to me, it's a tad embarrassing."

And then he began making references to colostomy bags and AARP cards.

"Obviously, that guy has never played golf," Watson says with a grim chuckle. "The game of golf takes physical skill. It takes mental skill. There is a tremendous amount of talent involved, even though they don't tackle you. You don't run, but you use a lot of violence in your swing, hitting the golf ball. Timing that violence with athletic skill consistently over and over makes it a sport."

Whether or not you believe golf is a sport—and, for the

record, *Popular Science* magazine actually proclaimed it was, by way of a serious study—those who aren't familiar with either the game or its tenets might indeed be asking, "Well, so what *is* the big deal about a fifty-nine-year-old man beating a bunch of youngsters at a game that requires no running, no blocking or tackling, or even heckling?"

It might best be explained by introducing you to the presumptuously titled Champions Tour, where Watson and the rest of those professional golfers over the age of fifty routinely make their retirement livings.

For twenty-three seasons, it was known simply as the Senior PGA Tour, which blossomed from a wonderful event called the Legends of Golf. The great old names of the game—Sam Snead, Miller Barber, Tommy Bolt, Gene Littler, Don January, and more—attracted huge crowds for that tournament even though they could not compete anymore on the regular PGA Tour.

And so, beginning in 1980, anyone over fifty who qualified could play on the new Senior Tour, sanctioned by the Professional Golfers of America. Arnold Palmer, Jack Nicklaus, Lee Trevino, Gary Player—a virtual Golf Hall of Fame—eventually would play in cities that rarely if ever hosted a regular tour event, and the response was electric. Some of them—Palmer and Nicklaus chiefly—would split their time between the seniors and the regular tour, but before long, all would escape to the land of the old-timers.

In fact, as the PGA Tour (the "flat-bellies," as they would become known, as opposed to those whose weren't) struggled to gain an identity until Tiger Woods graced it with his presence in 1996, the seniors set records both inside and outside the gallery ropes.

In truth, watching the seniors was a bit like looking in a mirror. It was a graying, faltering, stabbing collection of men who for the most part were aging right before our eyes. Their backswings grew shorter and their putting strokes were often a painful lurch. But they would look toward their faithful and offer a smile of chagrin and then sign autographs for hours in apology. They were us, our heroes in decline, Supermen in orthopedics, and we absolutely adored them for it.

To them, the Senior Tour was a vacation first and a second chance. And, as the Champions Tour, it remains just that today, regardless of what it's called. A vacation for those whose children are grown and gone, a chance for a man's wife to join him on tour for weeks at a time for the first time in his career. Some wives even carry bags for their husbands, much to the muttering of the old caddies who still search for regular work. Other men have their sons and daughters loop, a chance to bond while making a living.

So, it is a well-paying vacation. It is also a first chance for the club professional who never tried the regular tour but who honed his game with just this opportunity in mind. Turn fifty and give the seniors a shot. And it would be a second chance for those journeymen on the regular PGA Tour who never quite made it, who think the Senior Tour can be a gravy train.

"I've seen them come and go," says Senior Tour communications man Dave Senko, who has worked the gray-haired tour for nearly two decades, "and it's amazing how some of them approach this tour. Some were real successful and expect that to just carry over and they discover it's not necessarily so. Others haven't been competitive in years and want to prove they still have game."

The Senior PGA Tour, which sounded its age, was renamed the Champions Tour in 2003, even though a fair number of its members never won any championship outside of a Friday morning Nassau. It still has, as its foundation, the greatest champions in the game's history and can call itself anything it wishes.

Perception.

"Calling it the Champions Tour," admits former PGA communications director Michael McPhillips, "was more favorably received by sponsors."

Once upon a time and not that long ago, being a "senior" golfer meant you were old and over the hill. In many circles outside the game, unfortunately, it still does. Being a "champion," on the other hand, means you have credentials that can stretch back as far as you would like.

Tom Watson had plenty of those, coming to the Senior PGA Tour with thirty-nine victories, including his five Opens, two Masters, and two U.S. Opens, one of only fourteen men in history to have won at least three of the four major championships. He lacked only a PGA to have been one of five men, at that time, with the professional career grand slam.

A senior? Perhaps. A champion? For sure.

The senior tour has changed not only names but also physiques and attitudes with the introduction of a new generation to its midst. Until Tiger Woods became a linebacker in a golfer's suit, the PGA Tour paid little if any attention to physical fitness. In fact, Arnold Palmer once told me if he had known how important stretching was, he would have won at least ten more tournaments. *Just stretching.* Imagine weight lifting, running, flexibility training, which the majority of both tours practice now.

"I think when this tour started," says Mike Reid, who won a Champions Tour major at the age of fifty-five, "it was sort of a well-provisioned rest home for aging pros, but it is a dang competitive tour now.

"It still was a little bit laugh and giggle when I turned fifty and made the transition. There were a handful of guys in the fitness trailer, but the range was vacant after every round. The guys who followed us out here, they are guns. These fellows are very competitive."

The term "flat-bellies" still is the reigning differentiation between the regular PGA Tour and the Champions, but it is no longer totally accurate. With today's emphasis on conditioning, there are nearly as many flat-bellies on the older tour.

That said, it is rare that a golfer's success after turning fifty ever defines his career, unless he is one of those unique cases who emerge from the pro shop and somehow win a few times as seniors. Even with the tumult that Tom Watson created at Turnberry, it was simply an addendum to a wonderful career already posted.

"Tom long ago secured his legacy in the game," said Jack Nicklaus. "This [the Open] would have been something to add to the top of the cake."

The Champions Tour can be a sweet deal for those who qualify. The tournaments are rarely more than three rounds, as opposed to four on the regular tour, and there is no cut, so they are guaranteed a paycheck of some size at week's end. They generally play two pro-ams every week, which allows them double the chance to win extra cash and build relationships with the kind of amateurs who can use the player's talents in other lucrative fields such as Monday outings and the occasional endorsement.

There are six four-round events—the five so-called majors and the Schwab Cup at the season's end. The rest are 54-hole tournaments that begin on Friday and end on Sunday afternoon.

But the gravy train runs on a very short track. More than 85 percent of the Senior Tour events over the years have been won by men between fifty and fifty-five. No one, as of the summer of 2009 when Tom Watson was nearing both his prize Open Championship and his sixtieth birthday, had ever won on the Senior tour past the age of sixty-three.

And thus the astonishment as Watson began his improbable, nay impossible, assault. But while most of the world's mouth was agape, Watson's peers beamed with pride.

"There is maybe a step down when you're talking about us," said Champions Tour star Jay Haas in reference to the over-fifty crowd, "but it's not that great. And I think what

Tom's doing makes more of a statement for the Champions Tour than it disrespects the PGA Tour. Any given week, you put our top twenty, thirty guys out there on the PGA Tour, and four or five of them will make a little run maybe."

"Just goes to show you some of us old guys can still play," said Andy Bean, a multiple winner on the Champions Tour.

"I was pleasantly surprised [by Watson's Open performance]," admitted Dow Finsterwald, who is eighty and playing in the Super Senior Division of the Champions Tour. "It's harder to stay at the top of your game every week as you get older. Some sustain, but it happens to everyone eventually. The Open is such a tough tournament and exposes a man's nerves.

"But this only displayed what a wonderful player Tommy is."

"It demonstrated for golfers and nongolfers alike that you just never know about life," says McPhillips, the Champions Tour executive.

"He gave us inspiration and hope—hope for the possible."

Thomas Friedman, a longtime friend of Watson's, wrote in *The New York Times*: "Of course, Watson has unique golfing skills, but if you are a baby boomer you could not help but look at him and say something you never would say about Tiger or Kobe: 'He's my age; he's my build, he's my height; and he even had his hip replaced like me. If he can do that, maybe I can do something like that, too.'"

Watson had his left hip replaced just ten months previous, on October 2, 2008.

Tom Watson, framed by Ailsa Craig, putting on Thursday. *AP Photo*

Watson watches as the Four Horsemen of the Open ride into the sunset. *AP Photo*

Watson celebrating his 50-foot birdie putt on the 18th green on Friday, one of two "no-brainers" on that day. *AP Photo*

Watson and caddie Neil Oxman share a quiet moment. *AP Photo*

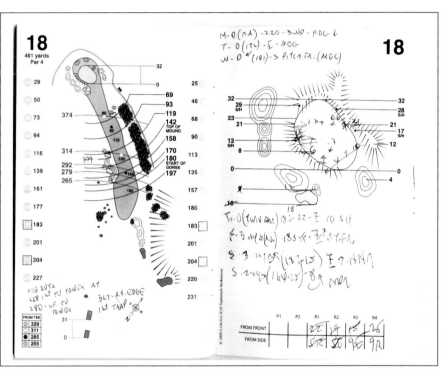

The actual 18th-hole page from caddie Neil Oxman's complicated yardage book used at Turnberry. *Courtesy of Neil Oxman.*

Tom and wife Hilary. *AP Photo*

Stewart Cink counts Watson's name five times on the
fabled Claret Jug as the legend looks on. *AP Photo*

Watson's second shot to the 16th green. *AP Photo*

"I could have lived with it for quite a bit longer," he told me, "but I did it because it was keeping me awake at night. I was tired of not being able to sleep. I was living with a bit of pain and, yeah, I was limping around, but I was fortunate because a lot of people in my same position have a lot of pain."

Friends saw a different level of anguish.

"I saw him a year and a half ago in 2008," recalls Chip Beck, an old friend and mate on the Champions Tour, "and he could hardly lift his left leg to slide over into a cart. We were in Japan playing. I asked him what was wrong and he said, 'My left hip is destroyed.' He was in terrible pain, it seemed. So what does he do but go out and get the hip replaced and six months later he's gonna win the British Open. Man is amazing."

"I started working out a couple months after the operation and started hitting balls in early January," Watson told me, brushing aside the procedure as just another bump in the road. "I think it took me probably until May or June to get my legs underneath me again, till I got my balance back. You add something new to your body and it creates just a little imbalance."

Factor into the Open equation, then, the fact that here was a man who was not merely battling the vagaries of age but still feeling his way back from hip replacement as he confidently made his way around the humps and bumps of Turnberry.

"At least it allowed me to sleep at night."

That would not last much longer.

1 3

DEALING WITH
FOCAL DYSTONIA

What happens to a man as he tumbles through midlife while holding a golf club in his hands? What makes his arms grow shorter and his hips turn to stone? This is, after all, a professional *athlete* (though the same people who argue golf isn't a sport would heartily disagree with that, as well) who has trainers and coaches and the kind of retinue that can mold and remold at the slightest indication of deterioration.

Lee Trevino, who split his fifty-eight career victories precisely down the middle between the regular tour and the seniors, watched from afar his old friend Watson at the 2009 Open with both scrutiny and admiration.

"The one thing Tom has going for him," says Trevino, "is right in the backswing. You know, as you get older, your shoulders don't move as well. That's why you can't hit it as far. He's got an upright swing but he can get his hands high. He still hits it a long way."

It is rarely, however, the first club with which a golfer chooses to play a hole but rather the last that succumbs to the vagaries of age.

"It's the putter," says Nick Price, who won the Open at Turnberry in 1994, a season when he triumphed six times and was PGA Tour Player of the Year. "I don't know whether it's a physical thing or mental. A neurological thing, perhaps. The brain tells the body one thing, but the body doesn't listen. Nerves. Yips."

Though the yips can come at any point in a golfer's swing and are not unique to golf but also to many other sports, they usually infect a golfer's putter. And it is not pretty. So many of the greats in history succumbed to the nervous, infuriating jab that almost seems spastic in nature. Ben Hogan and Sam Snead, for two. Snead reached a point where he tried nearly every putting style he could imagine to make his hands work: sidesaddle, between his legs, eyes closed. Bernhard Langer went through, by his calculations, four bouts of the yips before finally settling down.

"It's like someone else has taken over," he says.

They change grips, they change putters, they change length of putters, they close their eyes, they move their heads, they try anything and everything because it is the club that makes the difference between winning and losing, always. And it is not only the senior crowd. Vijay Singh, in his thirties and early forties, changed his putter almost by the round.

Despite winning twenty-three tournaments after the age of forty, he never seemed to develop a long-term relationship with that particular instrument.

If the long putter—which supposedly takes the right hand out of the swing and thus cures the yips—didn't work, he would go back to the regulation-sized putter the next day. And, though prominent in his struggles, he was far from alone.

Others believe it is more the man than the utensil.

"It's the Indian," Fuzzy Zoeller loved to say, "and not the arrow."

Unlike any other sport, however, the putter remains the ultimate nemesis. Imagine sluggers changing bats every game or bowlers changing balls. Imagine quarterbacks changing their passing motion or shooting guards switching their shots.

But visit a professional golf tournament and stop by the putting green early in the week. Notice the number of new-fangled putters stacked like kindling just tempting a struggling pro. Surely it can't be the stroke. It has to be the weapon. There are stories galore about men who have randomly chosen an old putter out of a barrel in a pro shop somewhere and then gone out and won with it. It *must* be the putter, then. Two weeks later, that putter is likely in a dark corner of the man's garage, there to pay penance for misdeeds.

Few veteran pros have gone through as many putters as former Open champion Mark Calcavecchia. He is famous for treating them like beggars. After one tournament in which he used a new putter very well, he laughed.

"It's earned bag time for a while," he said of the new weapon. "A while" turned out to be a week.

Stewart Cink, young and strong and capable, found himself turning to the long putter, sometimes called the belly putter, at an early stage of his career.

"Funny," he told me, "I always thought only guys who putted bad used long putters. If you showed up at a tournament with it, you were admitting you were a poor putter. But when I saw my coach with one, I thought, 'Well, maybe I have this all wrong.' If he thought it was a better way, then maybe it would free me up for a change.

"I resisted, but after a stretch of bad putting, I thought I would take a shot, and sure enough, I started having a bit of success with it. I had a couple good seasons. All along, though, I always thought of the belly putter as a crutch. I always wanted to get out of it. I wasn't ever satisfied using it. Some players think it should be banned, and, in a way, it all kinda bothered me."

And so in the weeks preceding the Open at Turnberry, after nine years with the belly putter, Cink made the change.

"I took a few weeks off to implement the routine that had been laid out for me," he recalls. "I was never a practice putter, but I worked harder in those two weeks than I had in two years. Mo [Pickens] said I had to find a way to practice where it means something. He came up with a great practice drill and a schedule for me. It was burning the routine into my mind. Soon, it began to really work."

The stroke, you see, never is thrown away, but therein usually lies the issue, especially for the older golfer.

And yet it does not necessarily confine itself to either the putter or age. Ian Baker-Finch, the affable Aussie known as the Dark Shark, was just twenty-nine when he won the 1991 Open at Royal Birkdale. The world rested at his talented feet when, almost suddenly, his game suffered a frustrating collapse. The putter, oddly enough, was the one thing that still worked well, his silky stroke remaining reliable. But within five years of winning the Claret Jug, he had given up the game, a victim of a driver gone terribly astray.

The most infamous, and painful, example of what went wrong with Baker-Finch came at St Andrews in 1995. Paired with Arnold Palmer in the latter's final appearance at the Home of Golf, with thousands watching, Baker-Finch stepped to the 1st tee and promptly hooked his shot so far left that it bounced out-of-bounds and into Old Tom Morris's Woolen Shop *off the 18th fairway,* a prodigiously poor and embarrassing gaffe.

After missing fifteen cuts in a row in 1995 and eleven more in 1996, he shot a 92 in the first round of the 1997 Open, a humbling score for a man such as this, and withdrew from the championship and promptly retired from golf.

"I've thought a lot about this," says Baker-Finch today, "and I don't believe mine was the yips. It wasn't a flinch, a reaction of the body. I simply had a problem when I had a driver in my hand and trouble either left or right.

"That drive on the 1st tee at St Andrews . . . oh, my, I hate that story, mate, but it's a pretty good example of what I was fighting. Huge crowd, pressure of playing with Arnold, cold, wind about forty miles an hour in our face, and here was my worst fear, having the longest club in my bag in my hand.

"Everyone on tour deals with fear of one sort or another. You see it a lot in chipping, almost more than in putting. Most times when you see a player using a putter from way off the green, he's facing chipping yips. Scared that he will chunk the first chip and then face another just like it."

Baker-Finch, bright and articulate, found a second career as a television analyst and, along with golf-course architecture and development, kept close ties with the game he loved without dealing with fear every day.

"I got to a point in the midnineties where I was just scrambling to make a cut, not even thinking about winning," he says. "I was trying to prove to myself I could play."

He was far from alone. Veteran well-known pros like Scott Verplank, Bob Tway, David Duval, and Jeff Sluman all fought the driving demons until they found something that worked for them.

Those who are cursed will try everything and anything.

A very talented young Australian named Peter Senior is a great example of that. He chips backhanded and uses a long putter that he anchors under his chin.

A decade and a half later, in 2008, Baker-Finch tested his game once more as he approached his fiftieth birthday with the Champions Tour in mind. He played two rounds at Colonial, missed the cut, but confirmed what he already knew.

"I found I can still play," he says, "and I also found that I can still make bad swings with the driver when I lose my focus. I'll treat the Champions Tour as a bonus where the stress is not as high."

Fear of failing is a mental issue. Flinching on chip shots and putts can come from deeper within the gray matter.

Researchers have labeled the problem focal dystonia, resulting from biochemical changes in the brain that accompany aging. They then get technical and describe the misfiring of neurons in the sensorimotor cortex, a thin layer of neural tissue covering the brain that is thought to cause contractions.

Yips.

Some pros compare the yips to a jolt of electricity just as they take the putter back. Others compare it to swinging a snake.

Putting and chipping demand such tremendous feel, and the palms and fingers are so integral to the club's control that any hesitation or misfire results in the ugliest of lunges. In earlier stages of research, amazingly, Botox injections blocked contractions in the affected muscles and actually helped. But remediation works better.

Tom Watson had the putting yips.

Bad.

For as many as ten seasons, during the prime of his career, he stabbed and jabbed and missed so many short and crucial putts that he estimates it cost him at least half a dozen tournaments, maybe twice that. In fact, he finished eleventh at Turnberry in 1994's Open behind Nick Price and attributed what he saw as a poor performance directly to his putting woes. Like everyone else (those who choose not to surrender and take up tennis), he worked diligently, smoothing out his stroke and accelerating through the ball. Easier said than done when one has focal dystonia.

"I still get nervous before I putt," he told me, "but by the time I'm actually standing over them, I feel confident.

"I still get the *nervouses*. In the '09 Open, I didn't feel too much pressure in the first round. Second round, a little more. Third round, very little. Fourth round, the most.

"Still, it was within the limits that I've learned how to deal with. I wasn't ever outside those limits. Not even close."

He is one of the fortunate ones whose hard work discovered a semicure. So many others, men like Hogan, Snead, Johnny Miller, and the great Harry Vardon, never did get over the yips. Vardon ironically was in Watson's headlights the entire weekend at Turnberry, for if Watson somehow managed to win, he would have tied Vardon for the record of six Open victories.

Concerns with the putter have never really left Watson. Instead of a practiced, unconscious stroke, it has become a very thoughtful struggle, especially with anything under ten feet.

"I have a tendency to yank it way inside and shut down the face," says Watson, the words of a man who has studied his art and worked on his failings for decades. "And I just can't get away from it. It's a quirk in my stroke. I . . . haven't resolved it yet.

"A longer stroke is okay. But one where I have to, you know, just take it back this far, well, if it doesn't go back straight, it just goes inside. So I've fought it for years."

At Turnberry, for the greater part of four magnificent days, he won that fight.

And so for the better part of one week in the summer of 2009 with hands high on the driver and a smooth stroke with the putter, Tom Watson shook aside the shaggy coat of age. It might have surprised everyone else, but not Watson or his faithful caddie Neil Oxman.

"Amazingly," said the man known as Ox, "nothing has happened age-wise to Tom. I believe he could really compete in five or six regular tour events every year right now, if they weren't eight thousand yards. Some say age takes a little off, but not Tom.

"If he putts well, he generally wins."

And at Turnberry, he was putting as well as anyone.

"As you know, the one thing when you get older is you get a shaky putter," said Lee Trevino. "But I saw a lotta putts from all over the place from Tommy at Turnberry. I think he had a great putting week."

He was not only putting well, his plan of attack was based on decades of experience in this land.

"The pros don't play links golf except in the Open Championship or the Senior Open," said Watson after Friday's round. "We [the older players] have played under these conditions for years and we kinda get a feel for it and that feel is worth its weight in gold when you're playing.

"So, no, I'm not surprised."

———

Neither were those who espouse the theory that it is the equipment, not the men, carrying the game into the twenty-first century. For decades, the argument has raged that better clubs and stronger golf balls have turned the modern golfer into a well-dressed automaton. Add in the enormous improvements in agronomy—men and women actually spend their college careers majoring in grass to turn today's golf courses into finely tuned playgrounds—and you have an argument that will never be won or lost . . . but will always be debated.

Fifty-nine-year-old Tom Watson versus thirty-seven-year-old Tom Watson is a case in the first point. One of the last times he seriously contended in a major championship for all four rounds prior to Turnberry (with every club in his bag working) was the 1987 U.S. Open at the Olympic Club in San Francisco.

"Twenty-two years later," wrote Mike Stachura in *Golf Digest* in the days following the 138th Open, "Watson's swing might look nearly the same, but his tools look like they come from a different sport."

His driver, an Adams Speedline 460cc in 2009, is an apple compared to a grape in 1987 when he carried a persimmon driver with a shaft that weighed nearly 140 grams, explained Stachura. His modern driver weighed 66 grams. And it was

45 inches long as opposed to 43 in the "olden days." And so what did that difference mean to Old Tom Watson at Turnberry? Nearly eighteen yards more than at Olympic. Considerably longer at fifty-nine than at thirty-seven. Granted, comparing driving statistics at an American Open to the British variety is not a fair judgment because of conditions, but the numbers seem significant still.

"Has anybody here taken an old persimmon head driver and hit it recently?" Watson asked before Turnberry. "I couldn't hit the sweet spot if it saved my butt. We have that big old thing now that, you swing it as hard as you can and if you hit it off center, it still goes out there. It makes you sloppy. The big-headed clubs make you sloppy."

Sloppy enough for a fifty-nine-year-old man to lead the Open over men forty-three years younger.

"If you're going to get a guy of our age to compete today," says Jack Nicklaus, "it almost has to be on a golf course that restricts the driver. Tom plays that little hybrid off the tee a lot and he plays it well.

"The metal driver also plays a big part in Tom's ability to compete. Wood driver? He wouldn't have been able to drive it that straight. At his age, he wouldn't have the strength to play out of that rough. Made a big difference."

Watson hit his driver only 60 percent of the time at Turnberry. The rest was left to the recent innovation that has helped turn the game around: the hybrid. He had an 18-degree hybrid and a 20-degree version in his bag that week, and he used them often and remarkably well.

"If there were no hybrids," Watson told me, "I'd be using a 2- or 3-iron off the tee. What it allows you to do is attack a course the way Tiger did at Royal Liverpool [in 2006
when Woods used irons off nearly every tee and won a very
emotional Open]. You take those bunkers out of play. You
take longer shots but you take the risk out for four rounds.
You take the risk out and you're gonna succeed at the Open
championship."

"A bigger, forgiving head with a much lower center of
gravity," writes Stachura of Watson's modern clubs. "Data
from Adams engineers suggest the center of gravity on his
hybrids is almost 25 percent lower than it was on his old 1-
iron," which Watson had in his bag at the Open in 1987.

———

The golf ball has changed dramatically, as well. But Watson,
for reasons known only to himself, chose to use a Titleist Pro
V1 from 2007 instead of the newer, more sophisticated Pro
V1x. Still, it was a dramatic change from the balata ball he
played in "the old days."

———

The question of agronomy would be laughed out of any pub
in Scotland. While it has certainly given the modern golfer
an enormous advantage on American courses where everything is groomed to perfection, such a thought becomes absurd in the Scottish realm where, although they have come
centuries in the care and feeding of their courses, they still

rely on the vagaries of the land, and occasionally on sheep as their mowers.

They have, after all, begun only in recent years to do laser marking on some of the major courses, distances from a sprinkler head to the center of the green. There are two factors involved; the idea of a sprinkler system in the first place is something very recent. Scottish courses depended for centuries on Mother Nature to water and on sheep to groom.

Offering measurements is a submission to the millions of American tourists who are so accustomed to the markings that, without it, the rounds tend toward the very tedious. It speeds up the game remarkably.

"Good golfers," says one old St Andrews caddie, "can smell how far it is to the stick. Bad golfers need numbers and then can't come close to hitting it that distance. I got to the point where I just hand 'em the club I think they should hit, forget the yardage. Here's a 5-iron, hit the damn thing, and forget it's only 135 yards.

"But when they're playing without us caddies, they have to have that yardage. So we gave in and marked the sprinklers for the Americans."

———

And so Tom Watson, with old and suspect hands grasping sparkling new equipment, with a mind that argued he was thirty again, summoned brilliance one last time.

His blue eyes hardened.

"Why not?"

14

"EVEN THE TALIBAN . . ."

Suddenly, Old Tom was news.

Tom Watson had not simply shot his 65 in the first round and then wandered off in ceremonial celebration, as most everyone expected. He had not followed it up with a mediocre Friday as he had in that tumultuous and teary U.S. Open of 2003, when Bruce Edwards, so sick already with ALS, was on his bag, and every bit of emotional energy was gone by the second day.

He sank the two no-brainers on Friday and got back to even par for the day and 5 under for the championship. He was staying right there at the top of the leaderboard and the world was anxiously watching. Oddly, it was not the first-round 65 that made the most noise but the second-round 70. Could he be serious?

Messages of support came from everywhere. Barbara Nicklaus sent yet another text message. *New York Times* writer Tom Friedman e-mailed him, "Even the Taliban are rooting for you." Friedman was in Afghanistan at the time, watching on Armed Forces Television.

Major Ken Dwyer, a member of Wounded Warriors, a foundation particularly close to Watson's heart over the years, messaged him to "forget those neck-high bunkers and four-foot putts. Go have some fun."

"Kinda puts things in perspective, doesn't it?" said a smiling Watson that afternoon.

Later, he reached back for the memories.

"While it was happening, I stayed in my little world. It didn't feel like I was transcending anything. I was just doing what I've always done, trying to win a golf tournament. But I started getting a pretty strong inkling what was happening outside my realm. My Outlook [e-mail service] stopped working. It simply broke down. It wouldn't accept any more messages. Friday, it just quit."

A moment of geek, if you will: There is no absolute number of messages allowed, but most individuals use .pst files in their Microsoft Outlook e-mail system that reach a tentative limit of two gigabytes (or two billion characters). If we assume that most of Watson's messages that week were an average of forty kilobytes in length, some larger, some smaller, it is estimated that his "mailbox" would hold no more than fifty thousand messages before crashing! That number is staggering to even the most computer illiterate among us.

————

The bookmakers were paying attention, too. From an opening-day 1,000–1 at the Ladbrokes in nearby Girvan, he would tee off late on Saturday in the third round at 25–1. Their early runaway choice, Tiger Woods, had sheepishly boarded his private plane Friday night and was home in Florida, having missed only his second cut in forty-nine professional major championships. He would pay little attention to the weekend telecast, working instead on fixing what ailed him.

The world wobbled, wondering what in heaven's name was going on. Its inhabitants had been dazzled beyond belief twelve months earlier when a similar feat of aging had taken this Open by storm at Royal Birkdale, on the western coast of England. A fifty-three-year-old Greg Norman, revitalized by his recent marriage to tennis great Chris Evert, was near the lead of the 137th edition going into the weekend, and the conjurers had visions similar to what they were now having with Watson. The latter, perhaps inspired a bit by what he had seen at Birkdale, was simply taking what Norman had attempted and stretching it to even more unbelievable lengths.

Norman, however, had stopped by Southport in 2008 only to warm up for the Senior British Open the following week. And he wouldn't have done even that had his new wife of three weeks not talked him into using the Open as preparation. On his honeymoon, at Skibo Castle in the Scottish Highlands, Norman grudgingly agreed and began to hit balls when a bell rang in his head.

"I remembered," he said, "that I used to stand closer to the ball."

How simple, yet it is around such rudimentary moments that drama occasionally revolves.

And so, with Evert gathering almost as much of the spotlight as he did, Norman used that swing thought at Royal Birkdale in some of the most brutal conditions in Open history. In a cold rain turned sideways by winds nearing fifty miles an hour, Norman let his blond locks fly and conjured memories of past greatness.

"I was nervous going to the 1st tee," he said, "and that's a good thing. I hadn't felt that way in ten years, maybe longer.

"Everybody has the chance to win this golf tournament. I made the comment at the start of the week that there could be a dark horse who would have a chance around here because of the way the course is set up.

"I'm sure there are players probably saying, 'My God, what's he doing there?' But I've played golf before. I've played successful golf before."

Though just a moment in time that he would not be able to repeat a year later, the echoes of Norman clearly hung over the air in Turnberry. The fact that the man known as the Great White Shark wound up losing on a brilliant Sunday afternoon to the Irishman Padraig Harrington might have lingered as well.

"A lotta guys later on in their career, their interests move on, their goals in life change," Harrington had said the night before the final round in 2008. "But Greg seems to be back thinking about it this week and he's well capable of putting it together."

Watson too thought of Norman's near conquest and knew age had nothing at all to do with what was happening. If you are in good physical shape and know how to play links golf, if you have the mental tools to face the daunting demands of what some feel is the toughest test of golf, who is going to tell you you're too old?

"Age is not a factor," says Lee Trevino. "Every one of us, that's how we get up in the morning, we think we can win. We hit this little ball, hell, it's gotta land somewhere, might as well stop by the hole.

"My wife told me years ago when I was gonna quit after winning the PGA in 1984, she said, 'Why quit? Your clubs have no idea how old you are.' She was right. Here I am almost seventy, still chasing that rainbow, still don't know how old I am."

"Golf doesn't have a number," says fifty-three-year-old Fred Funk, "not like other sports. Flexibility is such a big thing here, control your nerves, hell, you can keep playing.

"'Course, I'm not talking sixty years old. No, that's phenomenal."

"Surprised?" returned Billy Casper. "Well, Norman did it the preceding year and some of those courses over there, the older guys can play. Especially men who have had a lotta experience over there."

Watson's caddie saw it from a very different angle. "You know, some guys can only hit one shape shot out here," said Neil Oxman, describing players who employ either a fade or a draw on their shots. "Tom has a normal tight draw, himself, but he works hard at going the other way when he has to. He shaped shots that week at Turnberry with brilliance. He took what the wind dictated, what he saw in the landscape. I never saw anyone else do that as well as he did."

————

I had. At least for one magical afternoon.

Samuel Jackson Snead, who had finished third in the PGA Championship at the age of sixty-two, was eighty when I visited with him at his home in Florida in 1996. We went to the driving range where he had practiced for years and where he still worked, dreaming of that day when he might challenge the youngsters again. In fact, his only golf came here at the range and early in April on a Thursday morning in the Augusta dew as he, Gene Sarazan, and Byron Nelson ceremonially opened the Masters. One swing with a driver and the three of them were gone. But their golfing acumen remained as young as their hearts.

"One of the big deals," Snead told me that day, "is being able to work the ball left to right, right to left."

That statement came roaring back to me during Watson's remarkable voyage at the 138th Open. Work the ball, work it.

Snead stood with a driver in his gnarled, weathered old hands that day.

"There's a house at the end of the range," he said from memory, unable to see it himself, his eyesight nearly gone. "Now watch; this one will start at the right side of the roof and end at the left side."

With that remarkable, ageless motion, he ripped a drive that drew just slightly, exactly as he had described, the ball turning at the chimney and dropping softly 260 yards away.

"Now, this one will start at the left side of the roof and end at the right." He chuckled, as if performing a parlor card trick. Thirty years old again, he took the driver to its perfect pitch and, as his faithful yellow Labrador retriever watched, performed as predicted. He never looked, for it would have done no good. He couldn't see at that point more than a few yards beyond where we were standing. He merely turned to me and smiled.

"That's the way to work the golf ball," he said in his wonderful drawl. "Ain't a thing to it. But that's the key to great golf, son. Work it."

He would have loved the way Watson worked the golf ball at Turnberry a decade later.

Age perhaps played a large role, then, in that part of Tom Watson's game in 2009 but only the part of the aging process that generates great experience and marvelous instinctive talent.

The man could work his golf ball.

15

A NEW OLD TOM

Golf is for life. You are never too young to start, never too old to play.

—Tom Watson, 2009

Tom Watson stood on the edge of the 4th green and stared into the distance where four horsemen trotted neatly in tandem along the beach that borders the southwestern corner of Scotland. Though the course bordered the sea, this was the only place where you could actually see the beach, and he seemed lost in his own special world as he leaned on his putter, his back to the crowd.

A slight smile split his weathered face. "Old Tom," he might have thought, "isn't this the juiciest of ironies? Here I am, 148 years after the original Old Tom made his initial mark. Here I am, twenty years older than Old Tom Morris was when he won his first Open Championship. Maybe if I grew a long beard, yeah, a long red beard and I would *really* be Old Tom."

He blinked into focus and turned toward the 5th tee, his remarkable mission still brewing.

Midway through the championship, a real "old" Tom was creating the kind of breathtaking headlines never seen before in golf's glorious history. Vanquishing men more than half his age, he was in the midst of what his erudite caddie Neil Oxman called "a redefining experience."

If he could hold on to this lead, and certainly, surely, almost definitely that would be impossible for someone his age, but if by some strange chance he could, he would become the oldest major champion in golf history by more than ten years.

Remember the pandemonium when his friend and rival Jack Nicklaus won the Masters in 1986 at the wobbly age of forty-six? That glorious moment remains one of golf's most astonishing achievements, performed by a legend considered well past his prime. In fact, it was a few printed words of precisely that accusation that supposedly gave Nicklaus the fire to win.

"It [the newspaper article] said I was dead, washed-up, through, with no chance of winning again," recalled Nicklaus. "Oh, I was sizzling. Washed-up, huh?"

Watson was nearly fourteen years older in 2009 and facing the same silent accusations, though no one had the audacity to put such thoughts in print.

When Julius Boros won the 1968 PGA Championship at forty-eight, it was thought to be the most impossible standard in all of sports. Boros, an accountant who didn't turn professional until he was nearly thirty, quietly won the PGA, and then played very competitive golf for another fifteen years. In fact, he lost a playoff at Westchester to Gene Littler at the tender age of fifty-five.

But marching in the shadow of sixty in what is arguably the world's most difficult golf tournament? Impossible.

———

The man known as Old Tom Morris, who won four of the first seven Open Championships in the middle of the nineteenth century, was Thomas Mitchell Morris Sr. He was quickly dubbed "Old Tom" because he competed regularly with his son, "Young Tom," and this made it easier for newspaper reports to write them apart.

Old Tom Morris, after all, was only thirty-nine when he won his first of four championships, somehow dividing his time as St Andrews's first greenskeeper, building clubs out of hickory, stuffing golf balls with feathers, designing golf courses over godforsaken, barren wasteland, and playing the occasional money match. A guinea here, a pound there. Life was not easy in those days, but for Old Tom Morris, life was good nonetheless.

Here now was this twenty-first-century Old Tom, summoning a kind of surreal magic and setting the world afire. Golf fans of all ages were transfixed, but his performance was reaching far beyond the game to an aging population discovering an old friend and a new hero.

———

The four horsemen moved gracefully through the surf toward the afternoon sun. It was easy to wax poetic at the sight, so surreal. If they were indeed the biblical Four Horsemen of Revelation—pestilence, war, famine, and death—they showed no inclination to disturb the history being written on the cliffs above them just yet. Perhaps they were instead the reincarnation of Notre Dame's four old heroes—Stuhldreher, Miller, Layden, and Crowley—taking advantage of what was obviously a pretty serious time warp going on in the area.

Instead, yellow vests warbling in the midday sun, they were simply members of the Scottish Guard protecting the precious coastline from any attack by sea. Though the world atop the nearby dunes seemed to beckon more peaceful times, it remained 2009 and always on the edge of a new threat.

Old Tom Watson, back ramrod straight, turned to the next task at hand, pulled the driver from his bag, and settled his piercing blue gaze on the 5th fairway.

16

THE THIRD ROUND: LORD BYRON SMILES

On Saturday, July 18, with everyone continuing their Collapse Watch, Watson was paired with Steve Marino, a pleasant American who was getting his first taste of links golf and obviously enjoying the flavor. Playing alongside Watson, however—he liked that view even better. At one point, as the gallery once again rained down its support, he turned to Tom and said, "You could probably be king of Scotland. These people love you so much."

Watson took the short walk down the steps from the hotel to the golf course that afternoon dressed in dark. The familiar black cap topped off a black golf shirt, covered with a navy blue windowpane sweater with the white Polo logo, representative of the Ralph Lauren brand he had endorsed for years. Before heading to the range to warm up, he slipped into black rain pants for protection. Just in case. The shoes were the same black pair he had worn the first two rounds.

If the outfit seemed somber, the mood was anything but. He smiled large and often as he made his way through the growing crowds lining the route to the 1st tee where Marino awaited. Their tee time was the last of the afternoon, and as Watson stepped onto the box, he leaned toward Oxman.

"I love my office," he whispered through a smile.

Conditions in that office had changed again. While the wind on Thursday had been virtually nonexistent, it howled on Friday at their back on the 1st hole. Saturday, it was steady from the right and, with the honors, Watson took a 5-iron for the second straight day and found the ample fairway. From 137 yards to the front, he hit 7-iron hole high left, and 2-putted for par, his first there after two opening birdies.

The 2nd hole was back into the wind, and he hit a 2-hybrid off the tee, into the right rough. From 166 yards to the front, he hit a 6-iron to the front portion of the green and 2-putted for par. Steadily, the nerves seemed to be holding.

The wind was at his back on the 3rd hole, but his driver found a fairway bunker. He pitched out and, left with 160 yards to the pin, he hit a 7-iron and made the putt to save par. It was his first save of the week.

The pin was only 7 paces on the front of the par-3 4th green, and Watson wisely didn't go seeking it, instead hitting a 7-iron 40 feet past. He 2-putted again for par, but it was far from routine. His second putt was a testy 7-footer. While the pressure did not seem to be bothering Watson, it might have

begun to rattle Oxman, who dropped his trusty yardage jour-
nal and watched the wind carry it away. A steward nearby
helped chase it down like an empty bag of crisps while Watson
was off to the next tee.

That yardage book was as valuable to Oxman as any exit
poll or voter survey ever taken in his other line of work. It is
a detailed collection of hieroglyphics that only he can translate. In it is every wind direction, every yardage, every club
for the entire tournament. He could go to the 8th hole, for
example, and recreate in a flash precisely what Watson had
done there for all four rounds and the outcomes.

"I have to keep it up," he says, "because, say, on Friday
Tom asks me what we hit here on Thursday, what was the
distance, what was the wind, all that. I only have to look at
my book to give him the exact numbers.

"I don't usually write anything until I get on the green
because I want to know exactly where the ball is compared
to the flag. Sometimes you're going so fast, you have to take
time to keep it, but it is a valuable tool for both of us."

Watson hit a driver on the 5th hole, but his 4-iron second
shot from 185 yards found the big bunker to the right. Once
again, he got up and down to save par. He stood even par for
the day and still 5 under for the championship, still there at
the top of the leaderboard.

The par-3 6th is a demanding drive because if you don't
carry the green precisely, a severe slope tends to shuttle way-
ward shots into a very difficult bunker on the right front.
Watson saw his 3-wood to the 211-yard hole slide into that

very bunker. For the first time all day, he could not get up and down for par, and so the first bogey dropped him back to 4 under for the championship.

He got the shot right back at the 7th, however; he hit driver and 2-hybrid onto the front of the par-5 green, and 2-putted for birdie.

"Every now and then, it works," he said about his putting. "It's just every now and then, but right now, it's working."

He hit a driver into a sturdy wind at the 8th. The flag was perched on the top ridge of a very difficult green, but his 2-hybrid rolled 20 feet past and he 2-putted for par.

Somewhere, Byron Nelson was smiling down on him. Lessons remembered. Let par be your friend.

Watson lost his way for a while at the picturesque turn. Downwind at the 9th, he hit a driver into the right rough once again, leaving him 123 yards to the front of the green. He hit a pitching wedge onto the back fringe, but he could not manage a 2 putt, dropping his second shot on the outward nine, turning in a 1-over-par 36. He hit five greens and four fairways along the route.

With the wind out of the left at the 10th, he hit two-hybrid off the tee and, with 194 yards uphill to the front of the green, he hit a 5-iron 15 feet past the hole, and 2-putted for par.

At the par-3 11th, with the wind off his left shoulder, he hit a 9-iron 152 yards, 20 feet short, but he managed to save par.

With the wind from the right on the 12th hole, he hit a

driver to within 106 yards of the front of the green, but then he missed the green short left and did not get up and down. The bogey dropped him back to 3 under for the championship, still very much in the thick of the fight. The conditions were such that no one seemed to be able to make a run at him, and the story continued.

At the 13th, he hit a 4-iron off the elevated tee, leaving himself 146 yards to the front and another dozen to the front-right pin position. His 9-iron came up short and left of the green, but he managed to chip up close and make his par putt.

Along the Saturday journey, Watson found time to make idle conversation with Marino, who was having problems in his initial links experience. He would play the weekend 11 over par and finish well off the pace. But for a few moments on a comfortable Saturday afternoon, he reveled in Watson's presence. Watson mentioned early that he recalled playing a practice round with Marino at the AT&T National two years before, a fact that seemed to stun Marino and at the same time give him immense pleasure. *Tom Watson remembers me?*

"Truth be told, you really don't have much time to talk on the weekend." Oxman chuckles. "The rounds go so much quicker because you're only in twosomes, because you're waiting on one fewer guy to hit. The field is half the size, the rounds are maybe forty-five minutes quicker. But Tom found time to chat a bit with Steve, and it seemed to make him feel really good."

On the 14th, Watson hit a driver into the left rough, leaving him 186 yards into a really stiff wind. He hit a 2-hybrid

and wound up a dozen feet short of the green, but he managed to get up and down for par, a gain of at least a half shot
on the field considering the difficulty.

Back downwind on 15, he found a bunker with a 6-iron,
and he failed to get up and down for par. The bogey dropped
him to 2 under par for the championship, bringing a whole
host of players back into contention.

At 16, however, he hit a 3-wood into the fairway. From
121 yards to the front and another 25 paces to the flag, he
stuck an 8-iron hole high, and he made the putt for birdie.
The roar could be heard on every corner of the golf course as
the galleries seemed to be hoisting the man on their shoulders and bringing him home. He was back to 3 under for the
championship.

He made it 4 under on the par-5 17th. With his driver,
he found the middle of the fairway, leaving him 240 yards to
the front of the slightly elevated green. He had birdied this
hole the opening round but had settled for par on Friday.
With a 2-hybrid, which was becoming one of the favorite clubs
in the his bag, he found the green and 2-putted from 10 paces
for his second straight birdie.

Because he was coming home, the crowds seemed to
grow with every step, and as he moved to the 18th tee, they
lined both sides of the fairway, two and three deep. Watson
took in the scene but refused to allow his emotions to over-
whelm him. There was work yet to be done. It was only Saturday, but then the thought crossed his mind: "It *is* Saturday

and I could very well be working in the ABC booth. But here I am instead in *front* of the cameras. What a strange game this is!"

He ripped that same 2-hybrid into virtually the identical spot in the light rough that he had found on the first two days, leaving him 187 yards to the front of the green. After a brief consultation with Oxman, he hit a 7-iron hole high right, and 2-putted for par. One-over-par 71 was his Saturday offering, leaving him 4 under for the championship and 1 shot ahead of the field.

"The man is an inspiration," wrote Paul Forsyth in the *Scotsman* that night. "Not only is he an example to the weekend hackers ambling towards retirement, he is a reason to take up golf in the first place, for in no other sport is it possible to play, and compete, for so long."

"The first day here," Watson said, laughing, after the round, "it was like, yeah, let the old geezer have his day in the sun, you know, with a 65. The second day you said, 'Well, okay. That's okay.' And then now, today, you kinda perk up your ears and say this old geezer might have a chance to win the tournament."

Months later, he thought back to this remarkable afternoon of golf.

"Saturday, I played with almost no nerves," he recalled much later, incredulously. "I'd been there before. It was just a matter of handling it, just a matter of my short putts going in.

"That's where I always notice the nerves most, where it

has affected me for the last ten to fifteen years. When I make a short putting stroke and it goes to the inside right off the bat. Just one of those quirks. Once upon a time, you did it easily. Now, it's a struggle for some reason.

"Overcoming it? I've been trying to discover that but haven't found a solution."

The men directly behind him by just a shot, Australian Mathew Goggin and Englishman Ross Fisher, were only a *combined* two years older than Watson, who had a daughter two years older than Fisher.

Though Watson claimed not to be thinking about history, there are few in the game any better versed on the subject. He was well aware of where he stood, both in the tournament and the books.

"I don't know what's going to happen," he said. "But I do know one thing: I feel good about what I did today. I feel good about my game plan. And who knows? It might happen.

"It will be something special if I do what I intend to do tomorrow."

And then he repeated his mantra of the week: "I feel, I guess, serene. For some reason, I didn't feel nervous out there. Even when I messed up a couple times, I didn't let it bother me and I made up for it coming in. I feel like my nerves are too fried to feel anything. Let's just kinda go with what I've got."

Stewart Cink, playing five twosomes behind Watson alongside Lee Westwood, matched Watson's 1-over-par 71 and remained 3 shots behind going to the final day. He struggled on the outward nine with bogies at 5 and 7, but came home in 1 under par, taking advantage of the very reachable par-5 17th once again.

Three behind and virtually ignored in the maelstrom of Old Tom's continuing charge toward history.

OFFICIAL SCORECARD
THE OPEN CHAMPIONSHIP 2009
TURNBERRY

Tom WATSON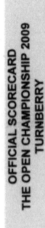

Game 37

Saturday 18 July at 3:00 pm

	FOR R&A USE ONLY	37.1	ROUND 3
36 HOLE TOTAL	135		54 HOLE TOTAL
THIS ROUND	71		206
54 HOLE TOTAL	206		

VERIFIED _C 7B_

ROUND 3

Hole	1	2	3	4	5	6	7	8	9	Out
Yards	354	428	489	166	474	231	538	454	449	3583
Par	4	4	4	3	4	3	5	4	4	35
Score	4	4	4	3	4	3	4	4	5	36

Hole	10	11	12	13	14	15	16	17	18	In	Total
Yards	456	175	451	410	448	206	455	559	461	3621	7204
Par	4	3	4	4	4	3	4	5	4	35	70
Score	4	3	5	4	4	4	3	4	4	35	71

Signature of Marker

Signature of Competitor _Tom Watson_

OFFICIAL SCORECARD
THE OPEN CHAMPIONSHIP 2009
TURNBERRY

Stewart CINK

Game 32

Saturday 18 July at 2:10 pm

FOR R&A USE ONLY		
36 HOLE TOTAL	138	
THIS ROUND	71	
54 HOLE TOTAL	209	

ROUND 3

54 HOLE TOTAL 209

VERIFIED C78

ROUND 3

Hole	1	2	3	4	5	6	7	8	9	Out
Yards	354	428	489	166	474	231	538	454	449	3583
Par	4	4	4	3	4	3	5	4	4	35
Score	4	4	4	3	5	3	6	4	4	37

Signature of Marker

Hole	10	11	12	13	14	15	16	17	18	In	Total
Yards	456	175	451	410	448	206	455	559	461	3621	7204
Par	4	3	4	4	4	3	4	5	4	35	70
Score	4	2	4	4	4	4	4	5	4	34	71

Signature of Competitor Stewart Cink

17

PUTTING IN
THE DARK

The magnificent Turnberry Hotel rests atop a hill overlooking the two championship golf courses, their clubhouse, and the Irish Sea beyond. In reverse, as the greatest players in the world playing the Open or the 30-handicappers on holiday make their way down the 18th hole of the Ailsa Course, the hotel sits almost as a crown over their heads.

If you walk out what is the back door of the hotel, startled by the remarkable vista before you, steps—ninety-nine in all—lead from the hotel to ground level. And there, between the bottom step and the road that fronts the golf courses, are a dozen seemingly innocent short holes, a par-3 course of the most unique measure. Guests of the hotel can choose their weapons and a few balls at the front desk, and entertain themselves into the wee hours below.

In the days after Tom Watson and Jack Nicklaus over-
came their fierce rivalry and became the closest of friends,
you could find them and their wives on this little course at
night after a few hours feasting, doing battle until they were
all rolling on the dew-laced grounds in fits of laughter. The
two men might have spent the afternoon playing for a championship across the street, but here, with little more than
wedges and putters, their nighttime wars were no less fierce.

Truth be told, the wives usually won. Smart men, these.

But on one occasion, their pitch-and-putt battle was used
as a not-so-subtle psychological boost for the yip-burdened
Watson. It was late Sunday night in 1994 after Watson had
limped home to be tied for eleventh behind Nick Price in the
Open. The Watsons and the Nicklauses were at it again.

"After a long dinner during which wine flowed," wrote
Jaime Diaz in *GolfWorld*, retelling Nicklaus's favorite tale,
one corroborated by longtime Turnberry superintendent
George Brown, who watched the scene from a distance,
"they had descended from the majestic hotel down to the
pitch and putt, which was bathed in moonlight as prominent
as the golden rays of 1977.

"They may have had their wives' purses slung over
their shoulders, but the moment carried an undeniable under-
current of poignancy. Nicklaus was exhibiting both empa-
thy and encouragement—friendship—to the very rival who
had handed him his most painful defeats. To insure that no
sentimentality would be betrayed, Nicklaus employed a
sharp needle.

"'Uh-oh, Tom's got a five-footer,' he said at one point. 'No chance now.' When Watson sank the putt in the near darkness, Nicklaus dug deeper. 'See how well you can putt when you can't see the hole?' Watson's gruff reply—approximately, 'You jerk'—was code for 'Thanks, I'll be all right.'

"It took awhile but he was."

With Nicklaus not there for the first time in their history together, Tom and his new wife Hilary spent a quiet evening Saturday and retired early to the suite named simply "Watson."

Nicklaus and his wife were forty-five hundred miles away this time. But their minds were quite clearly on their old friend. Nicklaus squeezed several sets of backyard tennis in between watching bits of the front and back nines of the Open.

"Like everybody else, including Tom," he admitted, "I had some tears in my eyes. He drove the ball beautifully and he hit some great golf shots and he is making putts when needed. If Tom plays smart golf tomorrow, he's the favorite. And I don't anticipate him playing anything but smart golf."

So many of the seniors talk about nerves and how they impact play. It doesn't affect only putting but also every portion of a man's game.

"We all have nerves," said Nicklaus. "But your nerve needs to overcome your nerves. That means you have to be nervy enough to do the things you have to do. That's what competition is all about, and Tom does a good job at that."

Nicklaus swallowed hard and considered his own eighteen major championships and the fifty-six times he finished in the top ten and what happens on Sunday afternoons.

"I just really hope he wins," he said. "I know Barbara and I will be rooting hard for him."

So would the world. The odds that were 2,500–1 in some books on Monday dwindled to a very manageable 10–1 as Tom Watson laid his head on his pillow Saturday night and tried somehow to sleep. Old men should sleep well. Old Tom? Sitting in the very lap of history? It would be a long but pleasant night.

———

Meanwhile, just 332 miles to the south, at a nursing home in Ovingdean, England, the world's oldest man died in his sleep that night. Henry Allingham was 113 years and 42 days old and, after being talked out of donating his body to science, he was cremated.

It is said he spent a good portion of his final day on this earth, July 18, 2009, watching the BBC's coverage of Watson and the Open Championship.

18

THE WORLD GATHERS

Neil Oxman is far from your ordinary tour caddie and so you would not expect him to share a tiny room in a house on the back road to Turnberry during Open week. It is not that he wouldn't, for he has considered himself a caddie first these last thirty-five years and that's what caddies do. It's just that, well, he doesn't have to. His "other" job as a political consultant allows him to travel in style.

And so he stayed instead for the week of the 2009 Open in the venerable but plush old Marine Hotel overlooking Royal Troon Golf Club, about thirty miles up the coast from Turnberry. He was on the second floor, ironically right across the hall from another Tom Watson suite, this one named in honor of the man who had won the Open at Troon in 1982.

It was comfortable but left Oxman a sturdy drive each morning down the A78, circling Prestwick where the first dozen Opens were held, and then offering the choice of the A79, the coast road, through Maidens and into Turnberry from the right, or down the A77 through Minishant and Kirkoswald to approach Turnberry from the left. He took the main road just once, on Thursday, and chose the coast road the rest of the tournament, leaving every morning at 4:30. The dawning light was dim and the ghostly outlines of rambling hills and large forlorn castles kept him company along the way.

Either way, Oxman made certain he left himself plenty of time. He never lost track of the old caddie axiom, "Show up, keep up, and shut up." Chances are good he overdid the first two but let the final admonition slide a bit. He and Watson not only walked fairways for a living but also shared their lives, e-mailing and texting often during off days about everything under the sun.

It was overcast and threatening rain, however, when Oxman arrived at Turnberry on Sunday morning, a good five hours ahead of the final tee time of the 138th Open Championship. Watson and Mathew Goggin were slated to go out together at 2:20 that afternoon, 9:20 on the American East Coast.

"I did all the things I had to do," recalls Oxman of that morning. "Cleaning grips and getting yardage, all my stuff, and still had tons of time.

"There were a couple easy chairs in the corner of the locker room and when I was finished, I sat down in one of them and fell dead asleep."

It had been a long and emotional week, and Neil Oxman was exhausted, with at least another ten hours of tremendous exhilaration to go. If he dreamed that morning, he doesn't remember.

"All of a sudden," he says, "I felt someone tapping my foot. Tom had quietly come in and was waking me up, not to go to work, necessarily, but just to talk. He sat down in the other easy chair.

"'Ox,' said Watson, 'I feel a little more nervous today.'

"I told him he deserved that," remembers Oxman, "but I also said to him, 'You know, for a lotta people, what you are doing is life-affirming.' I took it from a story about when Betty Comden and Adolph Green, who wrote *Singin' in the Rain*, showed Leonard Bernstein that famous scene with Gene Kelly. Bernstein said to them, 'That scene is an affirmation of life.' What Tom was doing was an affirmation.

"I said to him, 'Hey, you're not obsessed with tying Harry Vardon, you're not into any of that other stuff. It's those other guys who should be nervous. What you are doing is redefining yourself. What they're doing is life-altering. Huge difference, and that should make them more nervous.'"

"That was a special moment," Watson recalls. "He was into how he felt. I was just thinking about winning a golf tournament. I was putting a game plan into place. If I can make three birdies and three bogeys, I will win the tournament. That was my game plan. I came pretty close to that in the third round." (In fact, he had four bogeys and three birdies on Saturday.) "Now it was time to do it in the final eighteen."

———

The world began to gather as this inspirational journey was about to reach its mountaintop. Jack Nicklaus sat in front of his television set with his family in Florida and prepared to do something he had never once done in his entire life.

"I had never watched a complete round of golf on TV," the greatest golfer of all time said later. "But I couldn't miss this."

———

Nick Price, who captured the 1994 Open Championship on these same Turnberry grounds, invited a few of his golfing pals from the club near where he lives in Florida, mixed up several potent batches of Bloody Marys—remember the five-hour time difference; it was breakfast with Tom in America—and Price prepared to take his buddies on a tour of Turnberry.

"They just figured I could offer some insight," Price said, although the layout had been significantly changed in the fifteen years since his victory there. "So we watched together."

———

Lee Trevino, who won back-to-back Opens in 1971 and 1972, parked himself alone on his living room couch and prepared to be inspired. He had finished a distant fourth at Turnberry in 1977, watching Watson and Nicklaus go off on their Duel in the Sun together, leaving him and the rest of the field in their dust.

"I don't watch much golf these days," he says, "only the four majors. They make a guy's career. If someone doesn't win a major, he's not a great player.

"I was trying to read Tommy's mind. I didn't think anyone was gonna shake him because the nerves were on the other foot. All he was saying was, hey, these guys are sweating this out, they can't let an old guy beat them. He knew that, he's smart, he's a Stanford graduate. I know he also might have been thinking the wheels are gonna fall off, but if they do, so be it. He gave it a helluva run."

———

Jeremy Kavanagh, who joined Watson for the Tuesday practice round after betting on Whaston, had predictably missed the cut but wasn't about to miss this final day. He walked outside the ropes with the thousands who were ready to lift Tom Watson on their Scottish shoulders that Sunday afternoon.

———

The old caddie who had put £10 on Watson down the road at the betting parlor in Girvan earlier in the week had late Sunday afternoon off. His man had played just good enough on Friday to make the weekend but had fallen prey to the Saturday winds and so had an early tee time Sunday morning. The caddie finished their round, took care of his man's clubs, did their usual business, and then hurried back out onto the course to watch history (and several thousand pounds of winning bet) be made. If he rubbed shoulders that afternoon with Jeremy Kavanagh, he didn't know it.

———

In the media center, Associated Press golf writer Doug Ferguson was rehearsing.

"At every major, I spend an hour or so the morning of the final round putting together a crib sheet for various possibilities, usually names of four to five contenders," he recalls. "Sunday at Turnberry was no different. I started with Tom Watson and took a deep breath.

"I went eight names deep. Cink in the seventh spot. (Angel Cabrera was eighth).

"When I started writing game stories at majors a decade ago, I sometimes would try to come up with a lead that I could rely on in case I froze on deadline. This would have been one of those 'freeze' moments because the story would have been bigger than anything I had covered. I kept thinking about it before lunch, after lunch, as Tom headed for the 1st tee. I don't mind telling you, I was nervous. This was a big, big, big story and as a writer, you don't want to blow it. To say you'd only get one crack at a story like this is an understatement."

The veteran writer, whose work appeared in more than fifteen hundred newspapers around the world, didn't believe Watson could win.

"Nevertheless, I was cranking out numbers and scenarios, and his section of notes was far longer than those of anyone else. Each detail made it all the more absurd—longest gap between first and last major (thirty-four years) or the idea that he would go from number 1,374 in the world to inside the top fifty just ahead of Davis Love III. Each one was an example of how this drama was really more like fiction. Stashed *that* thought away, too."

———

Jeff Babineau, vice president, editor, and columnist of *Golf-week*, had a different assignment from Ferguson because of varying degrees of deadline. Still, the task ahead loomed just as large.

"With Watson going for number six," says Babineau, "and being nearly sixty, he was going to be a big part of our magazine lead *and* our lead column regardless of the outcome. Our average reader is fifty-plus, and a lot of them have followed Watson for many years. The other element/factor reminded me of Van de Velde in '99—it's so big and is such a huge part of the overall story of the week, you really can't write too much of it, in our opinion. Did people leave Carnoustie in '99 talking about Paul Lawrie? Not a single one. This was a similar day, where Watson, win or lose, would carry the tournament.

"That's why I was going to walk the whole way with Watson. I knew if someone else won, that part of the story would be covered by our lead writer, and I just wanted to keep an eye on Watson on what could be a truly historical day in sports."

———

Brendan Gallagher of the *Telegraph* was having trouble deciding where this would all rank not just in golf history but universal annals.

"You couldn't move over the weekend," he wrote, "without being reminded that it was exactly 40 years ago that Neil Armstrong stood on the moon, and frankly Watson's assault on the Open Championship just two months shy of his 60th birthday has the same feel of venturing into unknown and slightly mystical territory."

———

The longtime voice of golf on the BBC, Peter Alliss, was preparing his thoughts for what might be the most important round of golf he had ever called.

"I've had the privilege and pleasure of watching Watson throughout his career," Alliss says. "He was always fun to watch because he was brisk and busy and competent, always with a half smile on his face and a kindly word for one and all. That's a persona hard to keep up for thirty years or more."

Alliss was the lead basso profundo in one of the most unusual and crowded sets in all of TV sports. Several years before, the BBC had created a rolling TV studio along the lines of a sleek, bay-windowed mobile home that was parked alongside the 18th fairway. The set holds as many as six commentators at once, but there is also a production studio and edit suite that, hooked up to a truck, simply moves from event to event.

One would think Alliss, would seem more comfortable in a waffled old booth with enormous headphones and a lip mic than in this modern setting. Inching his way gracefully

toward eighty, perhaps he saw in Tom Watson his own golfing heritage as he looked back on Turnberry.

"Rounds one, two, and three passed and, dammit, he
was still near the top of the leaderboard," the former English
Ryder Cupper recalls. "In the commentary box, we specu-
lated as to whether he could do it. Would it be a good thing if
he did win? But this was all speculation, for it surely couldn't
happen."

———

On Sunday afternoon at 9:20 a.m. Eastern time, 2:20 local,
Old Tom Watson finally stood on the 1st tee, dressed in a
black golf shirt, a powder blue V-neck sweater with the Polo
insignia on the left breast, black slacks, and black golf shoes.
His black baseball cap had "Adams Golf" stitched across the
forehead, a relationship that goes back a decade. It appeared
to be, in fact, the same cap he wore the three previous days.

Some argued that Adams missed a golden opportunity
of creating a special Sunday cap or at least quickly building a
television commercial to take advantage of this enormous
moment. But it simply underlines what has been a partnership built over the years on quiet respect and admiration.
Adams, a small company out of Plano, Texas, has long called
Tom Watson "the face and heart and soul of the company,"
and he has never let them down.

Their publicly traded stock, to that end, rose by 18 percent in the hours following Watson's opening-round 65 and
another 9 percent over the weekend. That it rose to only

$2.85 a share tells you something about not only the size of the company but also the state of the golf industry in 2009.

The volatile American economy was taking its toll on golf at every level, from the professional tours to the private and public courses. New club openings were at their lowest in twenty years. And some of those men and women who once had the discretionary income with which to play the game were spending that on food and clothing.

At the very time of Watson's dramatic, emotional run at the Open, the Ladies Professional Golf Association was going about the ugly task of firing its commissioner in the wake of tournament collapses. Word spread that the LPGA could play as few as ten events on American soil the following year. Longtime sponsors weren't losing interest but losing principal, facing the same kind of decisions as the average golfer. Do we spend $5 million to sponsor a women's golf tournament or do we use that money to keep our economic heads above water?

The commissioner, a tough, hard-edged woman named Carolyn Bivens, supposedly had not made things easier, reportedly demanding long-term contract renewals and ignoring the enormous warning signs. A collection of the top players on the LPGA Tour got together in one very private and stormy dinner session in Toledo on July 2 and decided to demand Bivens's resignation.

On the Monday of Open Championship week, a gigantic ocean away, Carolyn Bivens stepped down.

Within a month, under interim leadership, several of the

sponsors who had tearily taken their leave actually changed their minds. "Long-term" became a year, perhaps two, instead of the four that was previously demanded.

The PGA Tour, while on much sounder footing, faced similar problems. Players anonymously groused about the way commissioner Tim Finchem was rowing their boat, and there were rumors of several tournament sponsors taking leave when their contracts were up. Finchem himself proclaimed rocky roads ahead, saying players would have to accept the fact that the economy was going to have its effect on their tour, as well.

The Champions Tour faced an even dicier future. So many of their tournaments are in small towns where the only industry is their sponsor. When that industry goes belly-up or takes thunderous hits, there is no one around to pick up the slack. Many companies use the tour to entertain clients and promote their products. One tournament has gone so far as to produce a software package that can track their guest attendees. But as a whole, the Champions Tour reflects the American economy far more precisely than does the PGA Tour because of its intimate nature.

The Greater Hickory Classic is a prime example. Held at the lovely scenic resort Rock Barn Golf and Spa in the western foothills of North Carolina for nine years, its splendor is a tremendous irony. Outside the gates, yards from its glory, rests one of the worst economic tragedies in America.

"Dunno how much longer they're gonna be able to afford that tournament," opined the general manager of a very popular local restaurant feeling its own pinch. "Our unemployment might be close to 20 percent in these parts. Folks are really, really hurting.

"We have nothing but the furniture industry here. Nobody is buying and so everyone's getting laid off. Heck, my wife has worked at one huge manufacturer for twenty years acquiring fabric. She used to work forty hours, maybe fifty, a week just buying bolts and bolts of the stuff. They couldn't build fast enough. Now she's lucky if she works twenty hours, buying for each individual sofa or chair. Imagine that? So how the hell are we gonna support some fancy golf tournament?"

The players who took part in the seventh annual Greater Hickory heard the usual applause from the small galleries, but they also heard the rumors. It was very likely there would not be an eighth. It seemed so incongruous. The lush, well-tended layout. The stunning homes, one of which sat atop a waterfall that tumbled toward the golf course. The hundreds of volunteers who had become like family over the years of their partnership. Could it be possible that in just a few months it would be no more because the area around it is destitute?

A man named Don Beaver, who made his fortune in nursing homes around the Southeast, had provided the majority of the bankroll for its existence. A Champions Tour event demands $2.5 million to be the title sponsor and another $1.5 million to make it a viable event. Beaver never flinched but had grown weary, according to reports, of being the tournament's primary source.

And who takes the most fervent hit when a tournament goes under? Not the players, who will wind up elsewhere. Not even the tour. No, it's the local charities to which every single tournament on both the PGA and Champions Tour donates 100 percent of its net proceeds. As Tom Watson stood on the 1st tee at Turnberry that Sunday afternoon, his and his compatriots' heroics over the years had helped donate more than $1.3 billion to local charities. The Greater Hickory Classic, for example, has a list of fifty charities that benefit from the tournament, everything from a local soup kitchen to the Boy Scouts.

So when a tournament collapses, it is the local hospital, the rehab and research center, the very sick and failing who have their protective carpet whisked out from underneath them.

A town doesn't have to be small to experience the economic punch. Ask Children's Healthcare of Atlanta, for instance. From 1989, when it became the PGA Tour stop's primary charity, until 2008, when BellSouth dropped the tournament and no replacement could be found, they raised more than $15 million. Another program, called Birdies for Charity, in existence for eight years, raised another $2.5 million.

The Atlanta area was a professional golfing mecca for decades. With the Masters starting the season down I-20 in Augusta, the PGA Tour stopped twice more, in Atlanta and in the Columbus, Georgia, area. The Senior/Champions

Tour had a steady presence until 2004, and the LPGA, though changing sponsors almost annually, still was a mainstay in Atlanta for more than thirty-five years.

Only the Masters and the season-ending Tour Championship remain of all that.

But as the professional game swirled in a summer of economic disarray, Tom Watson could hear only the resounding welcome as he and Neil Oxman picked out a spot on the 1st fairway for their opening tee shot, on their way to history. Only four and a half hours, only eighteen holes, only some of the most remarkable landscapes and breathtaking views, only a casual stroll along the cliffs of western Scotland awaited them.

Only immortality.

19

"INVITE THE CHALLENGE"

They were poised on the horizon like so many Indians in an old Western, ready to strike down the old man. Some were hardened veterans like the steady, placid South Africans Retief Goosen and Ernie Els, both of whom had major championships on their résumés and thus knew the pressures of Sunday with everything on the line. Others, like the Englishmen Ross Fisher, Lee Westwood, and the gangly young Chris Wood, were still waiting their turns.

Westwood was becoming one of the haunted, his glimpses of major victory routine and painful. He had come within a shot of the U.S. Open playoff between Tiger Woods and Rocco Mediate in 2008, and now here he was in the pack once again, sensing perhaps that his time was growing overdue.

There, as well, was Stewart Cink. The aches and pains of whatever had crept inside his tall, lean body over the past week remained to haunt him. And yet despite the fact that the bookmakers had reduced his odds to 16–1 going into the final round, he was sailing along quietly. As the AP's Doug Ferguson's list indicated, here walked the seventh option in most minds.

"It's something I'm used to," he said later, chuckling. "I've always been a guy who flies underneath the radar. That week with Watson sucking up all the oxygen, I think the only other guy who got any attention was Ross Fisher with his impending birth, you know, will he or won't he leave the course to be with his wife."

As Cink was playing, the words of his sports psychologist Mo Pickens rang in his ears. Every day, the same text message arrived, over and over again:

"Invite the challenge. Great routines. Stay patient."

One indication of how Cink was spending his twelfth Open was the serious lack of conversation emerging from his Twitter account. One of the first athletes to get involved with the popular social Internet page, quickly gathering over a million followers, his tweets that week seemed few and far between.

"May have swine flu. You'd think all the pork barbeque would have given me immunity," he wrote early in the week.

"Best weather I've ever seen in 12 British Opens," he posted on July 16, the day of the first round. "And best course, too. Now back at the room trying to get some air to circulate."

Two days later, at 6:47 in the morning, he tweeted, "Ninth tee at Turnberry the coolest setting for a tee anywhere. Sea, rocky coastline, castle ruins, lighthouse, and wind."

In all, he sent no more than ten of the intricate messages, kept to a maximum of 140 characters by page rule, through Saturday night. In contrast, at the PGA Championship in Minnesota a month later, he would send that many an hour, keeping his followers up to the moment with his thoughts and deeds.

"I consider myself a roaming observationalist of the world," Cink says with a laugh. "If I see something funny, like the condom vending machine in the clubhouse locker room, that goes on Twitter. A picture of number 5 at Augusta that no one else gets to see. That kinda stuff.

"It's lonely on the road and this keeps me busy. I have fun doing it and, on a professional level, it's hard to get our personalities out there into living rooms unless you're Tiger or Anthony Kim, Phil, sorta oozing charisma that most of us don't have. So we figure out the best way to be effective is to bottle things up. That isn't exciting.

"Twitter gives me a chance to get my personality out there and I can still perform at my best on the golf course. It's given me confidence to know that people care about what I say. There are a lotta people who support me out there.

"The one thing I have tried to do is keep it personal and not corporate. I try to promote without being too in your face and I think people respect that. If I go on a spree about a tournament or Tiger, I will get a lotta responses.

"I enjoy it and it's fun."

On Sunday evening at Turnberry, however, the stream

of tweets would increase dramatically as he shared with the world the most remarkable feat of his career.

He had spent most of the week right on Watson's heels and, like everyone else, was intrigued by what he was witnessing.

"The story was unbelievable," says Cink. "I'm not a scoreboard watcher in that I need to do this or that. But I'm always curious to see who is playing well. If somebody is having a good round, I use that as confidence that it can be done, that it's not impossible.

"We teed off about the same time on Thursday, in the morning. Because of what we shot, we stayed pretty close to each other every round. It was fun to watch him. I never saw any of him on TV but I knew he played well on Thursday, fell back on Friday before coming back. Saturday he fell back early. It was great. His name would disappear and then come right back to the top of the scoreboard.

"I think most of us were thinking, 'Well, a lotta guys have a hot start before falling back.' So every time he would fall back, I thought, 'Well, oh well.' It was remarkable though that he just kept coming back."

Stewart Cink's emotions were probably very close to those of each and every man who shared the leaderboard with Watson.

"It would have been easier to pull for the guy if you were in fiftieth place than if you were two shots back of him," says Cink. "I would have been perfectly content if Tom had won. It's easy to root for guys like that."

2 0

THE FINAL ROUND:
THE SANDS OF TIME

The enormous yellow scoreboard to the left of the 18th green on Sunday morning spelled it out precisely.

Tom Watson's name was at the very top, as it had been so many times over the decades. Mathew Goggin, Watson's playmate this final day, was tied with Ross Fisher just a shot behind. Lee Westwood and Retief Goosen were tied two shots off the lead. Jim Furyk and Stewart Cink rounded out the last of the seven men under par going to the fifty-fifth hole.

Very few, however, besides immediate families, had their eyes and their prayers on anyone other than the old Man. He had already won this precious event five times over a thirty-four-year span, but the last one had been a quarter century ago. Could he hold up? Could he somehow patch together one last brilliant afternoon of links golf? Could twenty thousand people hold their breath for four hours?

When Tom Watson's 4-iron shot found the middle of the first fairway, you could almost hear the gust of exhalation from the gallery. And with that, he was off on a ride that resembled the most wicked roller coaster at Blackpool.

Thirty-five-year-old Mathew Goggin had not won in a decade anywhere—and that was on the Nationwide Tour— was alongside Watson. He had been paired with Watson in the third round of the Open at Royal St George's in 2003. Until this moment, that had been his best Open experience ever.

"Tom is such a great player and such a great champion, especially at the British Open," Goggin said. "And it's just shocking how good he is. I mean, it's ridiculous. I'm thinking he's getting on in years and not playing so much, and he's just smashing it around this golf course. I am really impressed."

The official observer, and there is one in every group, was Jim Remy, the newly installed president of the PGA of America.

"It was truly an incredible day," Remy told me later. "It was so nice to see Tom smile as he walked onto every tee and every green. Even though he was in the middle of battle, you could tell he was enjoying every minute.

"It was one of the greatest experiences of my professional life, just being there."

———

The 1st hole on the Ailsa Course is a fairly straightforward wide-open par 4 measuring 354 yards, a good starter. There are nine bunkers, four down the left side of the fairway, one on the right, and another four guarding the green.

Playing into the wind, Watson found one of those to the left of the green and could not get up and down for par. A bogey right out of the chute and he fell quickly out of the lead. Meanwhile, Ross Fisher, whose wife was expecting their first child at any moment back home in England, birdied the first hole to take a 1-shot advantage. Would he leave the course in the midst of this, as he had promised, if the baby called? There were some who suggested his caddie should toss the cell phone and beeper into the Irish Sea. It remained, however, in the golf bag and quiet.

All eyes were on Watson. Had he merely teased the world those first three days? Was the opening bogey a sign of things to come, or would it be nothing more than the similar blips on his radar screen along this same stretch on Friday? Curiously, the watching world somehow seemed to be preparing itself for the worst. Surely this would be what most feared but expected as the pressure swelled and the nerves frayed. Was it imagination, or was he beginning to look his age for the first time all week?

The wind, steady at fifteen miles an hour but erratic in direction, changed from the time they moved from the 1st green to the 2nd tee and suddenly was at their backs as they stared down the 428-yard par 4. Watson chose a 2-hybrid off the tee and found the right rough. He was left with 160 yards to the front with the pin on the left side another 20 paces, hanging on a delicate slope. He hit a 7-iron some 25 feet past the hole and calmly 2-putted for par.

Once again on the 3rd tee the wind changed and came around a bit into their anxious faces. Watson hit a driver and had 160 yards to the front of the green, which slopes from front to back. Figuring the wind, he hit a 5-iron and, in golf parlance, was double-crossed, landing it over the green. He failed to get it up and down for par and wrote down his second bogey of the day. The lead was gone and Ross Fisher took the top of the boards.

"Really, at number 3, it was a lack of preparation or a lack of memory," Watson recalls much later. "My second shot, I have to remember I don't hit it to the right side of the green and expect it to stop. That green is very fast and the ball goes through very fast and, maybe due to nerves, I just forgot my strategy. I was kicking myself in the butt for forgetting."

At the tough par-3 4th hole, Watson chose a 7-iron for the 171-yard carry, left it hole high on the right and 2-putted for par.

But just as quickly as the affable young Fisher climbed into the lead, he let it slide away in one hole that perhaps is as indicative of the Open's hidden torture as any. At the par-4 5th, playing in the twosome directly in front of Watson, Fisher used an iron off the tee supposedly to avoid trouble, but threw it right, into the long hay near some troublesome gorse bushes. By the time he finally reached the green, he was facing a quadruple-bogey 8 and might have been wishing for that phone to ring. It took him from the lead to even par.

Watson stood on that same 5th tee and felt the wind in his face once again. Unlike Fisher, he hit a driver, and the ball found the middle of the narrow fairway 178 yards from the front of the green. His 4-iron stopped just on the right fringe, and he 2-putted from there for par. Paired with Fisher's debacle, Watson was back in a share of the lead, this time with Lee Westwood. That would not last long, but it was enough to offer Watson's fans some hope that perhaps he might have enough guile left to tiptoe around this devilish layout one more time.

On the par-3 6th, Watson hit a 3-wood to cover the 212 yards to the front, avoiding the dangerous bunker on the right that had led to a bogey on Saturday. He 2-putted for par to maintain his share of the lead.

Meanwhile, up ahead, Westwood continued to give British fans hope with a thundering eagle on the par-5 7th, and the lead was his. It was a remarkable day, with the lead changing hands nearly as often as the wind changed direction. Watson, Westwood, and Fisher all had the lead alone at one point or another as the afternoon progressed.

"I didn't have much time to think about anything except what we were doing," says Neil Oxman, "but for one infinitesimal split second there, I looked at a leaderboard and thought, 'Oh, well, maybe this is finally Westwood's time.' From watching TV and reading the papers, he had obviously been playing good coming in. The week before, he had lost in a playoff to Martin Kaymer for the Scottish Open at Loch Lomand.

"I had that really quick thought and went right back about my work."

The temperature hovered near 58 degrees, made chillier by the constant wind off the coast of Ireland just 175 miles away. The sun, however, offset the bitter breeze and the final-round tension made the chill almost unnoticeable.

The crowd inside the gallery ropes following Watson seemed nearly as large as the spectators on the outside. Among the followers was former Open champion Tom Lehman, who had finished his own final round earlier and, at the urging of his son Tommy, went back out to cheer Watson on. Writers, broadcasters, technicians, and fellow players all knelt in the thick Scottish rough at each hole to allow the paying customers their view of history.

If Watson was suffering from any nerves this day, it surely wasn't affecting his play off the tee. Whether with the driver or his favorite 18-degree hybrid, he was as deadly as he had been all week. From the middle of yet another fairway, he found the par-5 7th green in 2 but, once again, his putt for eagle was short. The subsequent birdie, though, lifted him back to 3 under par, a shot behind Westwood.

At the par-4 8th, his second shot found a hollow to the back right of the green, and he was able to get up and down to remain 1 over for the day and 3 under for the championship.

A cartoon in the July 25th issue of *Golfweek* had a desperate Father Time inside an hourglass with his hands blocking the sand. As Watson is nearby putting, Father Time calls out, "Hurry up, Mr. Watson! I can't hold this back much longer!!"

It was the very thought running laps around the minds of the world on this magical Sunday. The sands of time seemed destined to escape.

Meanwhile, Stewart Cink was playing very steadily. Though both American and British television showed very little of his play through the final round, clinging to the more popular story line, he was going about his business, staying close to the lead.

"Right where I wanted to be." Cink laughs. "Letting everybody else take the pressure."

Watson hit a 2-hybrid into the right rough on the par-4 9th hole, as he had the previous three days. He had 136 yards to the front and another 27 to the flag, and he left his pitching wedge short. He could not get up and down, racing his putt for par past the hole. At least, mumbled his critics, he got that putt to the hole, which he hadn't been doing on most of the outgoing nine. He had hit five out of seven fairways, missing only the 2nd and the 9th, but he managed only four greens in regulation. His putting, though unspectacular, was steady; not a single 3-putt. (He went the entire championship, in fact, without a 3-putt, which is usually the one Open statistic that underlies a runaway winner.)

Westwood, in front of Watson, bogeyed the 10th hole but maintained his 1-shot lead over Watson and the bearded Mathew Goggin, who became lost in the midst of the tremendous turmoil surrounding Old Tom.

Two hours left. Nine holes over some of the toughest landscape in all of Kingdom Golf.

Those thoughts might have crept into Tom Watson's mind as he and Oxman stood at the 10th tee. Chances are, however, this might have been an opportunity to sneak one last glimpse of the old lighthouse just to the left. Who knows, it could be the last of their lifetime, certainly of their Open Championship tenure.

The glance by Watson took all of a few seconds, for he had been this way before, and his focus turned quickly to the middle of a treacherous fairway that demands a perfect tee shot. He chose a 2-hybrid with the wind helping out of the left off the sea. His approach was from 168 yards, and he hit a 7-iron five paces past the hole from where he 2-putted for par. Mathew Goggin, however, birdied it and moved into a share of the lead, back in the mix again.

———

"I was giving my pals a guided tour of Turnberry," recalls Nick Price, who was sitting at home in Florida watching every moment on ABC. "Every hole, I would tell them where Tom should be hitting the shot, the best advantage into the green, all that. You know what? He was never more than a yard or two away from where I was telling them. It was an amazing run. To have that control, wow, just astonishing."

———

At the par-3 11th, he had 173 yards to the flag, which was essentially in the middle of the green. His 9-iron shot was a little short of hole high, leaving a 15-footer for birdie.

Near the green, his old friend and ABC announcer Andy North turned his back to the green to shield his words from the competitors. "Every time Tom has needed to make one of these this week," whispered North, the two-time U.S. Open champion and Watson's partner in one of the Champions Tour's team tournaments, "he has."

And sure enough, for the first time that day, Watson raised his putter slightly toward the sky as he watched the birdie fall. He was back in a share of the lead with Goggin and Westwood, and back to 1-over for the afternoon.

At the 12th, however, Watson's driving accuracy came a cropper as he pulled his shot left, where it hit a woman in the shin and bounced into the long rough. With a strained smile, Watson signed a glove and gave it to the woman, sheepishly apologized, and went back to the business at hand. He was left with 170 yards to the front with the flag 24 paces on the back right. He hit a 4-iron into the fringe and made a steady 2-putt par.

A half dozen holes to go. Six on the way to history.

———

Announcers checked their notes. Writers fiddled with their leads. It would not be half as memorable if the man simply ran away with it, right? It had to have some drama to match its romance. He has not played particularly well, has not putted great, and yet here Tom Watson stands on the steps of the Temple of Perpetuity. The gallery, blue-faced from holding its breath, challenged the man to continue his climb.

Oxman said nothing except "172 to the front, 190 to the hole, wind from the right." He would not allow himself to think about anything else.

"Yardage, shot, divot, yardage, shot, divot," Neil Oxman repeated. "That was all I had time for. And it's probably a very good thing."

At the par-4 13th, Watson hit a 4-iron off the tee with the wind at his back, which left him with 158 yards to the front and a healthy 35 paces more to the flag. He hit 8-iron to the right of the hole, and he left his birdie putt short, settling for par. As someone said later, "He would have been four shots ahead of the field if you gave him an ounce of extra power on every putt."

While Westwood was cruising along in the lead, seeming to fit Neil Oxman's earlier assessment, Watson hit a driver into the wind at the 14th, his ball finding the right rough, wispy fescue that was really nothing to be concerned with. He hit a 2-hybrid to within 15 yards short of the bunker that guards the green. After good par putts on 12 and 13, he left himself 10 feet for par on the 14th. His putt was not short, give him that, but it grazed the edge of the cup and stayed out. The bogey dropped him back to 2 under par.

Westwood found himself in trouble at the par-3 15th. After driving it into a bunker, he played a poor second shot and wound up with a 20-footer for par. He missed that and fell back to 2-under par. Watson stood on the tee box and watched it happen. He was back in a share of the lead.

"My feeling down the stretch," recalls Watson, "was being fortunate to be in the position I was in. Players were making a lot of mistakes. I was, too, but they were keeping me in the tournament. I still had the game plan in mind. I said, 'All right, you have to make three birdies, two bogeys, the rest pars.' That was the plan, and if I did that, I'm right there.

"I had a great group out there, the crowd. The people were pulling for me. That kept the whole day in perspective. I had my plan and I was trying to stick to it."

At the 15th tee, he watched events play out in front of him, someone in a bunker, another in the rough, the advantage of playing a virtually flat links course where you could see several holes ahead. Many players don't pay attention to scoreboards, would rather not know where they stand. Others need that information for emotional balance. Scoreboards are on every hole at the Open and are hard to avoid. But with his targets only a few hundred yards ahead of him on this final day, Watson had all the kind of knowledge he needed. When it came time for him to hit, he turned to Oxman for the rest of his input.

"Okay, 184 to the front downwind," came the report, "31 into the green with the flag at the back. Remember, you don't want to be in that back bunker."

Watson hit a 7-iron about 5 paces short of the green. He chose putter, making two good veteran strokes to get his par. It was all he wanted at that stage.

The theater played out ahead. Westwood hit it long and over the 16th green and failed to get up and down for par, falling a shot back now of Watson.

Old Tom stood on the 16th tee and assessed his situation. He had played the last three holes through the week
at 5 under par without a single bogey. They had once been
considered far too easy for finishing holes, and so in the 2008
Open, designers were called in to make them some of the
toughest on the Open rotation. Tough and memorable.

The 16th was rerouted from a straight fairway to a dogleg right, bringing the stream that runs in front of the green
and along the right side more into play. Forty-five yards were
added to its length.

In all, Turnberry was 247 yards longer than it had been
for the Open in 1994 and had twenty-one more bunkers. But
it could have been much worse. The original redesign added
more than one hundred new bunkers, but it was decided the
changes were too penal and another reworking was demanded. Still, a far different and more challenging layout
faced the men of 2009.

And as he stood on the new 16th tee, Watson had the lead
by a shot. Stewart Cink, Mathew Goggin, Lee Westwood, and
the wild-haired young British manchild Chris Wood were all
right behind him.

He hit a 2-hybrid off into the left rough.

"We had a discussion there," recalls Oxman as they
faced the second shot. "What to hit, 7 or 8? I was worried
that he make sure he carried enough to get over the water."

The shallow Wilson's Burn, basically a ditch carrying a
stream of water that wanders beneath the front of the green
and up its right edge, makes the approach shot daunting.

Once on the huge green, life is not that much easier, but it was here in the second round that Watson made one of what he called his two "no-brainers" that day, a 60-foot putt that never strayed from its course. On Sunday, he was only 35 feet away for birdie, but left it 4 feet shy. Goggin made bogey to fall back to even par for the championship.

Watson stood over the 4-footer. It was precisely the distance that had haunted him through his darkest putting period, the kind that makes the right hand jerk and the head turn for assurance, and the toe of the putter peek right just enough to push it off-line. Steadily and calmly, with lips pursed, he rolled it pure and got his par. The gallery recognized the turmoil, knew the man and his history, and loved him dearly for it. The noise was deafening.

Westwood, playing the par-5 17th, somehow escaped a bad lie in the rough and played a magnificent second shot to within 20 feet for eagle. He missed that but settled for a tap-in birdie to regain a share of Watson's lead.

Up ahead at the 18th, Stewart Cink faced a 15-foot putt for birdie. Was the memory of that tragic day in 2001 at Southern Hills in Tulsa when he had missed the short putt that would have gained him entry into a playoff still with him this day?

"I think it stuck with him, I do," his caddie Frank Williams told *Golfweek* later. "You had to wonder."

Cink, who had gone from the long putter to the belly putter to the conventional putter and all the way back, pushed everything negative out of his mind. He putted immaculately the entire championship and wound up second in the field with an average of just 1.854 putts per hole. He had been tied for first in putting after his opening-round 66, tied for ninth after the second round, tied for thirty-eighth when Saturday was finished, and through the stressful final round, he managed 30 putts to tie for thirty-second. Certainly one of the better overall putting performances of his career.

And certainly made all the more impressive by the fury that churned inside the man who feared he had swine flu.

But now there was one left, one gigantic tumble across the green that surely looked twice its 15 feet.

With the crowd sensing the importance of his putt, Cink settled the bill of his green Nike cap over the ball and made one of the purest strokes of his championship.

"It was a big moment," he recalls, "no question about it. I knew I hit a great shot in there, 9-iron from 197 yards, and although I didn't know that the putt was to win the British Open, I just knew it wouldn't hurt.

"Just before the putt, I kinda laughed and asked Frank, my caddie, if now was a good time to abandon my preshot routine. He laughed and said no, don't think so, just do that routine and knock it in the hole.

"I was very calm. It was like a putt on the practice green back home."

His friend and psychologist Mo Pickens spoke of the moment in the first person as he watched from his home in South Carolina.

"I just had the most important putt in my life," said

Pickens, "and I hit it without any fear whether it would go in or not."

The birdie earned Cink a momentary tie for the lead, there for the first time in four days, out of seeming nowhere. Though he had hovered near the lead on Thursday and played steadily after that, he never was envisioned as a contender until . . . he was.

The crowd's reaction was, to say the least, mixed.

"I teased him a little," said Williams. "I said, 'I liked that putt, but I might have been the only one who liked it.' Tom Watson's their hero. We knew we were the bad guys."

Watson had no idea what had happened ahead. Playing the relatively straightforward par-5 17th, with a 22-mile-an-hour wind dissecting the fairway, he hit a driver into the thin right rough. He had 235 yards left to the front of the long, narrow green and almost the length of the green to the pin. His 2-hybrid shot ripped through the green and into a hollow behind it.

He chose to putt up the hill the remaining 20 feet for eagle.

"It's the safe play," whispered ABC's Andy North.

And it was the best play, settling within a few inches for the birdie that got him back in front of Cink by a shot.

"The emotions were in check," Watson remembers. "I had to separate myself from them, and that's just what I always do. If I'm playing well, I try to use those emotions, but I have always had the understanding that you can't let the highs of a great shot dictate your next one. Same thing with a bad shot. You can't let the lows affect you. I have always had the ability to recover. They call that Bounce Back on the tour. You make bogey or double bogey, well, what happens on the next hole? How do you deal with that? I've always been pretty good about that."

In fact, in 2009 on the Champions Tour, he managed to bounce back nearly 21 percent of the time, thirty-third among his peers.

Meanwhile on this fateful Sunday, Mathew Goggin was falling to even par and out of the championship. All who were left were Watson by a shot over Cink and Westwood.

The latter missed the 18th green to the left and, over a large hump, zipped his first putt 6 feet past and missed the comeback to fall frustratingly to 1 under par. He was looking to become the first Englishman since Nick Faldo in 1992 to win the Open, and the pressure was enormous. Just the summer before in the U.S. Open, he had missed the Torrey Pines playoff with Tiger Woods and Rocco Mediate.

"It's gone from frustration to sickness," he said after leaving the 18th green at Turnberry. "This is the Open Championship, and it's the one that means the most to me."

Watson meanwhile stood on the 18th tee. One hole left. Two swings, hopefully, two putts, and a sixth Claret Jug, tying Harry Vardon for the most Opens in history.

One bookmaker had Watson's odds at that very moment at 1–10, overwhelmingly in his favor.

Fifteen minutes at the most.

A quarter of an hour to immortality.

2 1

EIGHT FEET FROM
IMMORTALITY

The professional golf world puts all of its focus primarily on four weeks a year. It is quite simple, really. Beginning on the second week of April in Augusta with the Masters, it skips May and proceeds to Father's Day week and the U.S. Open. Almost precisely a month later in July, there is the Open, and in August the PGA Championship completes the Holy Quadrangle. These have been the majors for nearly half a century.

It is difficult to determine exactly how this foursome took on that lofty status, but most believe it blossomed in 1960 when Arnold Palmer, taking the golf world by storm, won the Masters and the U.S. Open and figured, "If I win the British and the PGA, that would make a grand slam similar to what Bobby Jones accomplished in 1929." Jones's slam consisted of the U.S. and British Opens and the U.S. and British Amateurs. Since Jones was a lifelong amateur, he could not compete in the PGA and, face it, he wouldn't create the Masters for another five years.

Other championships have come along, offered much more prize money, claimed far better fields, but these four moved into the standard lexicon and have remained entrenched probably forever as the four major championships.

As Tom Watson stood on the 18th tee late on Sunday afternoon, ready to claim his sixth Open, a great many critics began to breathe a huge sigh of relief. Perhaps, they thought, the world was about to right itself at last.

The first two major championships of the 2009 season had been tales of what might have been. Forty-nine-year-old Kenny Perry had the Masters in his pocket before bogeying the last two holes that fateful Sunday and losing in a playoff to the Argentinian bear Angel Cabrera. Had Perry hung on, he would have eclipsed Jack Nicklaus's mark as the oldest Masters champion by some three years.

Two months later on a rain-soaked muddy public course, the ferocious Bethpage Black on Long Island, David Duval, once the number-one player in the world but having slipped disastrously to 882, saw his last-hole putt lip out on the final hole that would have earned him a U.S. Open win. No comeback in history would have been as stirring.

In his wake, the popular left-hander Phil Mickelson was playing the tournament only at the behest of his wife, who was resting in a hospital bed three thousand miles away, battling breast cancer. His mother, astonishingly, was suffering the same fate.

"Amy asked me to bring home the trophy," Mickelson said, early that week, "to put on her bedside table."

He missed two par putts in the final four holes and wound up in second place behind an unassuming little-known youngster from South Carolina named Lucas Glover.

It is not that either Cabrera or Glover did not deserve their championships. They took what they were given, earned what they received. It was simply a case of what might have been. The galleries might not have wished it nearly as much as the media, intent on writing history and documenting tears.

So in the third major championship of 2009, the memories were still very fresh. Watson would more than make up for what had been denied the historians. Just like that, they would forget Perry's collapse and Duval's lip out, for this surely would be the greatest story in golf history, no, in *sports* history.

The last time the Open was played there in 1994, the new 18th hole on the Ailsa Course was nearly 30 yards longer than in 1977. Bunkers were put in place on the left side of the fairway, directly in the golfer's landing area, and to the left and right of the green.

Watson stood on the tee box, hands on his hips, as Neil Oxman ran the numbers, just as he had for the seventy-one previous holes. His voice was steady, nary a hint of the nerves that surely bubbled beneath the surface.

"Two hundred and fifty-eight yards to the right TV tower," he told his boss. "Two hundred and eighty to the one on the left."

Watson did not hesitate, immediately pulling the same 18-degree 2-hybrid from his bag that he had used the three previous rounds at the final hole.

"I knew I had a 1-shot lead," Watson says. "All I had to do was put the ball in the fairway one more time. So I hit my hybrid like I had all week."

"He was supremely confident in his tee ball all week," Oxman said later, "whether it was a driver or the hybrid. I think he hit that 18-degree club twenty-four, maybe twenty-five times during the week."

Watson swung the club for rhythm once and then let it settle behind the ball.

In the seconds that followed, as the white tee catapulted over and over toward the front of the tee box, the ball arched through the crystal blue Scottish sky and landed almost precisely where his tee shots had the first three rounds, on the right side of the fairway near the TV towers.

"With that tee shot splitting the 18th fairway," recalls the BBC's Peter Alliss, who had a front-row seat in his mobile studio next to that fairway, "the championship was in his grasp! Unbelievable."

"When he found the middle of the 72nd fairway," said Nick Price, "I knew he had won it. That's the hardest thing, hitting that fairway."

"Absolutely perfect," reported ABC's Andy North, who had moved down the rough line along the fairway for a better advantage and would rapidly walk toward the green to follow Watson's ceremonial march to history.

Stewart Cink sat in the scorers' cabin, watching the event unfold on a small television.

"I had decided not to clean out my golf bag when I was finished," he said, "a bit of reverse psychology. But when Watson hit the fairway at 18, I was like, oh well, this was a great experience. Once he hit that fairway, I thought I had lost my chance."

Watson had 189 yards left.

"It's a number I will never forget," says Oxman, the caddie and political consultant, almost shuddering at the memory. "Our actual yardage was 164 to the front plus the pin was 25 for 189 to the hole. It was 196 to the back of the green.

"Lost a congressional race once by 85 votes out of 270,000 and a Senate race by 5,124 out of 1,284,811. Never will forget those numbers, either."

Adrenaline probably doesn't factor into politics, but in golf it must be considered. Swinging the very same hybrid club, Watson had 206 yards left in the first round, 204 in the second, 202 in the third, and now just 189. He and Oxman had decided on a 7-iron each of the first three days and accumulated two pars and that no-brainer birdie on Friday.

It was also a 7-iron in the final round of the 1977 Open to within 2 feet that helped Watson beat Nicklaus in the famous Duel in the Sun at Turnberry.

This day thirty-two years later called for a different decision.

"Ox, what are you thinking?" Watson asked. It was precisely 6:19 p.m.

"I'm thinking 8."

"So am I," answered Watson.

It was a call that will haunt the both of them for the rest of their lives.

Oxman churns through the numbers like a frustrated CPA. "The carry onto the green is an extra 4 paces because you've got the elevated green. You've got 4 to the front and 7 in the middle and 10 on the right as you go slanting on a diagonal to the front side to carry on up on the green. You need to carry up to the green on the right side. It's an extra 10 yards. So in fact, the real carry to the front of the green was 170 yards.

"Question was . . . and you're not saying this out loud, you're computing it . . . if you hit a 9-iron, are you able to carry that 170 yards?"

He went on, a recalculation that will ramble through his wizened mind as long as numbers make any sense.

"I was trying to hit it 164 yards," Watson said later, speaking as only veteran golfers can when they talk distances. Most golfers talk in generalities; pros talk in specifics. "And I hit exactly the shot I wanted to hit, I really did."

He could see it playing out in his mind. Using the wind, he would nip the ball off the tight fairway grass and let it hit no more than a foot on the front of the green. It would then have the full length of the green to roll out, hopefully stopping within a dozen feet or so of the flagstick.

Taking the 8-iron lightly in his white glove, he settled his weathered right hand comfortably into the same grip that had served him so immaculately all these years. The world held its breath. You could literally hear the breeze, it was so quiet.

Slowly he took the club back and dropped it confidently behind the Titleist. The thump split the Sunday evening air as the clubface made contact, a spit of brown turf flew forward, and the ball rose into the brilliant sky. It seemed to hang there for the longest of time.

"I hit the shot I wanted and, when it was in the air, I thought, 'This may be mine,'" said Watson.

"I never saw a replay," says the Pennsylvanian Oxman "but a Philadelphia TV station slowed the shot way, way down and they say he hit precisely right on the front of the green. It just hopped on him."

Watson, with the advantage of months of hindsight, played the shot again in his mind for me.

"It was blowing very hard at my back. My instinct was to carry the ball 164 yards to the green. I felt that an old 8-iron was the right play, it could hit a little bit short but would be perfect. If it landed at the front edge, it would stop and be right there.

"The reason I didn't hit 9-iron was, well, I didn't think the chances of me hitting the green were that great. I couldn't carry that 9-iron 170 yards in the air. If I mishit it a little bit, it might do funny things, like with Jesper Parnevik."

In the final moments of the 1994 Open at Turnberry, Parnevik failed to check a leaderboard going to the 18th hole. He thought he needed to be aggressive when a par would win, so he hit too much club into the final green and wound up bogeying the hole and losing to Nick Price by a single shot.

Watson could not blame lack of knowledge. He knew precisely where he stood and what he needed to win.

"I couldn't afford to have happen what happened to Jesper," recalls Watson now, "so I just hoped the best decision was to hit 8-iron, and I did."

———

Peter Alliss was on his feet in the BBC booth, electricity surging through his old bones. "He struck that second shot beautifully and whilst it was in the air, I thought to myself, 'Dammit, he has done it!' "

But he hadn't.

The ball jumped as though it had hit concrete and rolled through the green and over, settling perhaps an inch into the thick rough that surrounds the green, 3 feet below the surface.

"The lie," reported Andy North, "is not great."

Hindsight came into focus immediately.

"People can second-guess it," says Watson. "Hey, *I* second-guess it. I should have gotten it on the green, not knock it over, but there wasn't any way I could've knocked a 9-iron over."

"If I had been his caddie," said Nick Price, "I would have had him hit short and right and let him 2-putt from 30 feet for the win. And I would have called for a 9-iron, but . . . he was really pumped up.

"So easy to say when you're not there."

Stewart Cink is a bit harsher. "I've been in the game a long time," he says, "and I know that when the pressure starts to build, you make mental mistakes. When Tom hit that second shot on 18 after a brilliant drive, his ball landed on the green. And that was a mental mistake. You can't land the ball on the green coming downwind like that at the Open. You just can't.

"That was my first indication that the pressure, that the whole weight of the week, was getting to him a little bit.

"When the ball fell over the swale behind the green, I turned to my caddie and said, 'Don't pack the bag yet.'"

"There can't be self-recrimination," Watson said. "I tried my best with every shot and sometimes you make the right judgments and sometimes you don't. If I had hit a 9-iron on the last hole, I may hit it three inches fat and come up 20 yards short. Who knows?"

"He hit a really good second shot," said Jack Nicklaus with a view from a Florida couch. "And he came about six inches from winning the tournament. The ball rolled into a very awkward place to get it up and down. It wasn't a mental error. It just happened."

"Shades of the olden days," said Billy Casper. "I think when he hit the second shot at the last hole, he would have given two million dollars for that shot while it was in the air. One of those things . . . must've been really pumped up."

"You can't hit two better shots in a major that you're leading by 1 than he hit," said Lee Trevino, from much the same vantage point as Nicklaus, thousands of miles to the west. "Beautiful 8-iron, caught a hard spot in the green, ran 70 feet over. Just as easily could have stopped 10 feet from the hole."

Neil Oxman, who had no issue with the 8-iron before it was struck, looks back in agony.

"I know that, on my deathbed, I will say, 'I should have pulled a 9-iron instead of an 8'"—he chuckles—"and then I will close my eyes and die.

"People say he hit the wrong club, wrong in the sense that it didn't work. You never know. I want to know what would have happened if we had hit 9. Where would the 9 have pitched, and would it have gotten us up there?"

"I wasn't totally surprised," says Watson. "That's the beauty of links golf—the surprise factor. You never know what will happen until the ball stops rolling. The wind, the firmness of the ground, it's what makes links golf so maddening. You might hit a perfect shot, but there's always uncertainty with the bounce."

"I felt bad for him," Cink says. "That was a weird feeling, a strange emotion. I felt very satisfied with what I had done. The negative part of me was like, I've put myself out on the line again, maybe a playoff now. But the other side of me was like, I can't wait to get back out and play. I felt I really had good stuff in my golf game."

Golf is a game of continuing accumulated results. One shot leads to another, and until you are finished, you aren't. So while Watson and Oxman stood dumbfounded behind the 18th green at the result of what both they and thousands

more called "a perfect shot," they had to put the result out of
their minds and move on. There was at least another shot,
hopefully only two more, left. In golfer's parlance, they had
to get up and down from a very tricky spot. If they manage
that, Watson becomes the oldest major champion in history
and the sports world shouts from the highest mountaintop
for a century to come. After all, he still had a 1-shot lead over
Stewart Cink, still had the Open in his veteran grasp.

"I was pulling for him so hard," said Champions Tour
mate and old friend Peter Jacobsen. "I was actually nervous.
I was shaking on that last hole. I wanted him to win it so bad,
I could taste it."

———

Watson had several options for his third shot. He could chip
it, hoping somehow to get the ball to stop in tap-in territory.
Or he could putt it.

He chose the putter.

"He played the shot he should have played from there,"
said Nicklaus. "If he tried to chip it, there was a chance he
could have taken a 6."

"I know that slope there," said Trevino. "How do you
chip it? If the lie is down in the grass and you bump it up the
hill, you're taking the chance of hitting it fat and the ball rolling back to your feet. He made the shot that was, percent-
agewise, the best shot."

"The lie dictates what shot you're going to take," Watson
told me. "The ball had just rolled into the short rough and

was sitting in that rough. The grass was sticky. I was playing with my back to the wind and my first thought was to pitch it. Then I said, 'Well, you know what, my best play is to putt the ball.' I could have pitched it and left myself with a 15-foot putt. I said if I putt it, the worst I'm gonna have is about a 10-foot putt. So I gave myself the benefit of the doubt. I played the odds that I was going to get the ball close.

"It's all in the touch and feel. I'd had that play a thousand times over the years."

The enormous gallery, which brought Watson home to the 18th green with fanfare worthy of a visiting diety, suddenly gathered its collective breath again. Not a whisper, not a sound.

"I know he paused," said Oxman about the decision to putt instead of chip. "I know when he's gonna use the putter. I don't even have to look at him, I can hear his decision. Right away, he takes his glove off. Well, he didn't take the glove off right away this time. But when I finally heard the Velcro, I took the putter cover off. He didn't have to say anything."

Watson looked quickly to Oxman with a grimace masquerading as a smile, settled over the putt, and let it go. The Titleist Pro V1 with the two black dots quickly climbed the mound, found the green, and rolled 8 feet past the hole.

Eight feet from history. Eight feet from immortality. Eight feet and move over, Harry Vardon. Eight feet that must have looked like eighty.

"I knew he was in trouble," said Lee Trevino. "Now for the first time, he was standing over a putt to win the championship. So now the age factor didn't come into play anymore, it was the putter in his hands. He will tell you. When you have a lotta pressure on you, you can't accelerate."

"He putted beautifully all week long," said Nick Price. "You know, I was pulling for him not because he was fifty-nine or because he was one of us but because he's done so much for the Open Championship, so much for links golf. I thought this would be his reward. Here you are, Mr. Watson, for all you've done, this is your reward."

His reward, however, was a cruel reminder of the years he labored in the putting graveyard. The seventy-first stroke of the day, the thirtieth putt, was weary, tired, by far his worst of the week. It never had a chance, sliding right of the hole.

"He just fanned it a little bit," said Oxman. "You're not gonna make every 8-footer. He putted lights-out all week."

"I was screaming at the television," remembered Trevino. "I was yelling, 'Take your right hand and put it underneath like you're gonna duck-hook it. That way, when the right hand quits, it keeps the putter square.

"Oh, man, I felt so bad for him, I really did. But I was still so proud."

"He just hit a bad putt," said Nicklaus. "In that type of situation, unfortunately, it's very excusable. You saw his expression after he missed the putt. It was like, 'Oh boy.' He laughed and that was it."

"It was a miserable putt." Watson laughs now. "I went through my routine, you know, for all the marbles. Do what you normally do. And I didn't do it. I got over the putt and didn't really get quick with it. I just blocked it with my left hand. It was a terrible putt."

Almost before the ball finished rolling, Watson raised his head and looked at the packed grandstand, a painful clenched smile his only comment. They looked down on him in agony, emotionally spent. As the ball came to a stop, they allowed themselves one collective mournful groan. If they could have given the man a hug, they would have.

"I smiled at the crowd in disgust. I said what a lousy putt that was. That's why I smiled."

Watson took his time and made the short comeback putt for bogey, his first of the week on any of the closing three holes, took off his black Adams cap and waved it to the adoring, heartbroken fans. He had not lost the Open yet, there still remained the four-hole playoff that is unique to the Open. It only felt like he had lost. So strange, considering the way he had just played the final hole of regulation.

He had hit a brilliant drive, his best of the week, and a second shot that landed precisely where he had aimed. His putt up the hill and back onto the unforgiving green was carried off nicely.

It was the putt for par, the putt for the Open Championship, the putt of dreams . . . and nightmares.

For one of the few times all week, the man had openly shown his age and everyone saw it, everyone gasped at the familiarity of the flailing putter, and with that, everyone suspected that there would be a far different end to this story than had been dreamed.

"A young Tom Watson would have made that putt and that may have been the difference," said Andy Bean. "Sometimes age does catch up with you. But for seventy-one and a half holes, my goodness, it was great."

The week had, as it always seems to when emotions and pressure are involved, dwindled in excellence for Watson. The number of fairways hit each of the four rounds went 12, 11, 10, and 8. The number of greens in regulation were 14, 12, 10, and 10. He had 28 putts in that magical opening round but finished with three straight rounds of 31 each.

Good enough, as it turned out, for overtime.

Watson and Cink for the Claret Jug.

"When I made the birdie putt at the last hole," Cink told me later, "I still would have been peaceful if Tom had won because I felt like I did what I could do."

But the rooting was over. There was work left.

"I was back into the adrenaline," he said. "It never kicked out on Sunday. Thursday, Friday, Saturday, I locked up and felt absolutely awful after the rounds. But Sunday I had that charge at the last hole, and with the playoff, well, I stayed up the entire time."

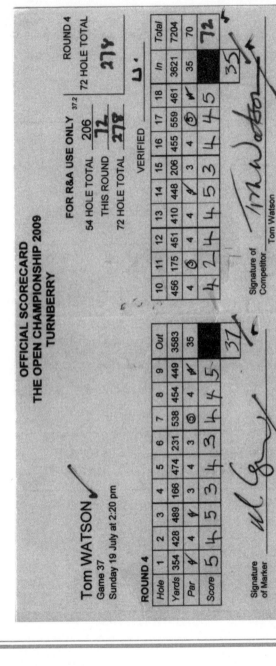

OFFICIAL SCORECARD
THE OPEN CHAMPIONSHIP 2009
TURNBERRY

Tom WATSON

Game 37

Sunday 19 July at 2:20 pm

FOR R&A USE ONLY

	ROUND 4
54 HOLE TOTAL	206
THIS ROUND	72
72 HOLE TOTAL	278

72 HOLE TOTAL 27Y

ROUND 4

Hole	1	2	3	4	5	6	7	8	9	Out
Yards	354	428	489	166	474	231	538	454	449	3583
Par	4	4	4	3	4	3	5	4	4	35
Score	5	4	5	3	4	3	4	4	5	37

Hole	10	11	12	13	14	15	16	17	18	In	Total
Yards	456	175	451	410	448	206	455	559	461	3621	7204
Par	4	3	4	4	4	3	4	5	4	35	70
Score	4	2	4	5	3	3	4	5	5	35	72

VERIFIED

Signature of Marker

Signature of Competitor _Tom Watson_

Tom Watson

OFFICIAL SCORECARD
THE OPEN CHAMPIONSHIP 2009
TURNBERRY

Stewart CINK
Game 34
Sunday 19 July at 1:50 pm

FOR R&A USE ONLY		ROUND 4
54 HOLE TOTAL	209	72 HOLE TOTAL
THIS ROUND	69	278
72 HOLE TOTAL	278	

34.2

VERIFIED

ROUND 4

Hole	1	2	3	4	5	6	7	8	9	Out
Yards	354	428	489	166	474	231	538	454	449	3583
Par	4	4	4	3	4	3	5	4	4	35
Score	4	4	4	3	5	3	4	4	4	35

Hole	10	11	12	13	14	15	16	17	18	In	Total
Yards	456	175	451	410	448	206	455	559	461	3621	7204
Par	4	3	4	4	4	3	4	5	4	35	70
Score	5	2	4	3	5	2	5	5	3	34	69

Signature of Marker

Signature of Competitor — Stewart Cink

22

THE PLAYOFF: THE
FINAL UNRAVELING

It was the ultimate in anticlimax. For four brilliant, inspirational days, Tom Watson had taken the calendar and turned it inside out. He had invited us aboard a ride no one had ever experienced before. In the end, or what seemed surely like the end, he had crashed us all. The air left our lungs and we, all of us worldwide, lowered our collective heads in the strangest of pain. We hurt for him, beyond anything else, but we also hurt for ourselves, for we once again discovered that sometimes dreams aren't meant to come true.

That there was a four-hole playoff left seemed almost meaningless. We sensed the outcome with the wave of that weary putter in the middle of the 72nd green. Could he somehow summon another hour of magic? It didn't seem likely. We (and *we* were in this together) were spent.

At the end of regulation, Watson and Stewart Cink were tied at 2-under-par 278. The playoff route would go from the

5th hole to the 6th and then across to the par-5 17th and home to the 18th. There is no strict routing for Open play-offs. It varies from course to course and depends more on convenience and the inclusion of at least one par 3, 4, and 5.

Each major championship has its own kind of playoff system. The Masters is sudden death. The U.S. Open is a complete eighteen-hole playoff the following day. The PGA Championship is three extra holes while the Open is four. There is no rhyme or reason, just individuality.

This was only the eighteenth playoff in Open history but the seventh in the last fifteen summers. In its formative years, the Open used a thirty-six-hole playoff on the day after the final round. The first of those came in 1883 when Willie Fernie beat Bob Ferguson at what was at that time one of the most revered nine-hole courses in the world, the Old Links at Musselburgh in East Lothian. Not far away from Muirfield and North Berwick, Musselburgh officially dates back to 1672, although there are those who claim Mary, Queen of Scots played a form of the game there nearly a century before that. Trapped inside a racetrack, the Old Links has been refurbished but was essentially forgotten as the Open moved on to eighteen-hole venues.

The thirty-six-hole playoff format dwindled to an eighteen-hole next-day event in 1970, and it was within that format that Watson defeated Jack Newton at Carnoustie in 1975.

The R&A decreed ten years later that a four-hole aggregate playoff made more sense, and Mark Calcavecchia won the

first of those over Wayne Grady and Greg Norman at Royal
Troon in 1989. In the years to follow, playoffs became almost
the norm, with the last one before Watson-Cink coming again
at Carnoustie in 2007 when Padraig Harrington defeated
Sergio Garcia.

And so, in the fine and lengthy sunlight of another Scottish Sunday evening, the Open sent yet another set of combatants back onto the course to settle their deadlock. Tied
now at 2 under par, Watson and Cink would play four extra
holes, and if they remained tied at the conclusion, they would
begin sudden death.

The adrenaline would have to act not only internally for
Cink but as a protective suit of armor, too.

"We knew we were the bad guys," said Williams. "Tom
Watson's their hero."

"I felt a little sorry for Stewart," said Lisa Cink. "But
then I figured he was at least going to be part of history and
he could use that as motivation to overcome."

Watson and Oxman reached the initial playoff tee first.

"I just told him, 'Hey, you've had one playoff here recently [the 2003 Senior British Open] and you won that, now
do it again,'" said Oxman. "That's all I said to him.

"He's very stoic, very even-keeled. When things are going well, yes, he can get a little excited, and when things are
going badly, he can get a little down, but it's never outwardly
off the norm. Because he knows he has to produce the next
shot.

"When a round is over and he's done really shitty—and

frankly, I haven't caddied for him very often in really shitty rounds—it's not like he slams around, but he's just . . . disappointed. If he's done something wrong, he goes out and tries to correct it. But he's very good about shaking things off. And that's where we stood going to the playoff. It was like, 'I'm out here and have to play these next four holes,' and that was it."

There was an edge in the air, palpable and dark. When the foursome finally met, Watson and Cink shook hands but said little. It had taken awhile for the proceedings to begin and there was talk that Cink was deliberately playing mind games, making Watson stew in his own juices. Instead, it was merely nature's call.

"We had to wait because Stewart had gone into the loo," remembers Oxman, "and the players' loo was about seventy-five yards away from the tee."

Finished, Cink made his way to the tee box, shook Watson's hand, offered his sincere congratulations, and waited to see who hit first.

"Tom had his game face on," said Williams.

"I was prepared to be the villain," says Cink. "I had a little talk with myself before the playoff. I knew the crowd was going to be pulling for Tom—they should be! He was the story of all stories. I just had to tell myself, 'They're going to be for him, you know how to play this golf course, you're swinging good, trust it. Just go out and do what you know how to do.'

"I also felt that the big finish, the birdie at 18, would

give me the confidence and was a contrast to the way Tom finished. I felt like I had a huge opportunity with extra holes and he felt like he had squandered an opportunity."

Watson was giving away nearly twenty-four years to Cink, but he had been doing that and much more the entire week to everyone in the field. Suddenly, however, the gap appeared blatant. The romance of the great adventure seemed to have disappeared, replaced by a sad cruelty.

Cink, like his wife and caddie, knew where he stood.

"Whether Tom was fifty-nine or twenty-nine, he was one of the field and I had to play against everybody," he said after the round. "I just play golf and I play it how I find it."

When Cink finally joined Watson, there was a brief rejoin. Ivor Robson, the immaculately coiffed, high-pitched Scotsman, stood ready. It was his first work in over five hours since the last group of the day had teed off. He had, hopefully, taken the time finally to refresh and relieve his system.

On the elevated 5th tee, with almost a larger gathering inside the ropes than out, Robson smiled, shook the hands of Watson and Cink, and said into his microphone, "Good afternoon, ladies and gentlemen, may I welcome you to the playoff to decide the winner of the 138th Open Championship."

Watson stood to the side next to Oxman, their eyes focused on some far distant object, perhaps a fleeting glimpse of what might have been.

Back at the 18th green, meanwhile, David Hill, the R&A's director of championships, had taken his own microphone and prepared to do a truncated play-by-play of the playoff action for the fans who remained in the enormous grandstands there.

A golf cap with two numbered discs was offered to the combatants by a member of the R&A. Watson, looking off toward the water, blindly reached into the cap first and picked 1. He would have the honor.

Watson had played the 5th hole warily over the four days with pars on Thursday, Saturday, and Sunday, and the lone bogey on Friday amid that tremulous stretch that threatened to derail whatever dreams he had forged. Cink, on the other hand, had parred the par-4 5th hole on his opening round, only to follow that with three bogeys.

Watson stepped up, waggled his driver, and striped a solid tee shot that found the left side of the fairway.

Cink, with an iron, followed suit.

The wind had died slightly in the early evening and, hitting first from the fairway, Cink's ball found the right bunker alongside the green nestled in the sand dunes. Watson had 162 yards to the front and another 27 to the pin. Earlier in the day, he had hit a 4-iron and his shot landed hole high; he 2-putted for par. In the playoff, he took a 5-iron, but his ball found the bunker on the left.

While Cink was able to get up and down for par, Watson left his sand shot about 15 feet wide and could not make the putt.

"Sometimes Tom's legs don't work," recalls Oxman, "I don't think on his second shot that his legs were working.

Maybe he was a little tired. They didn't work as well as on the tee shot when he drove through hard on his legs."

Cink suddenly had his first lead of the week. As strange as that may seem, it was hardly without precedent. When Angel Cabrera won the Masters in a sudden-death playoff nearly four months earlier, it was his first outright lead of the week, as well. It doesn't matter how you get there, the old saying goes, just that you're leading when you do.

They moved on to the par-3 6th called Tappie Toorie (Hit to the Top). While Watson had bogeyed the hole two of the four rounds, Cink had birdied it on opening day before playing it even par the rest of the way.

With the honors now for the first time, the six-foot-four Alabaman's shot found the green from 227 yards.

Watson hit his 2-hybrid and pushed the ball right.

Dead.

In fact, one blogger who was doing Internet play-by-play said it looked like the perfect place in which to dispose of a body.

Watson and Oxman stood at the bottom of the large hill on which the green was situated, wondering how in the world they might handle this bit of trickery. Watson's hands were on his hips, his head down. Oxman stood to the side, lost in thought. Watson had used a 3-wood earlier in the day to within 20 feet and made par. This was a whole different task.

Watson took a sand wedge, settled comfortably over the Titleist, and somehow lofted the shot neatly onto the surface of the green, 8 feet from the hole. Nearby, inside the ropes and watching from above, veteran pro and former Open champion Justin Leonard applauded. It was difficult to determine just where his emotional loyalties lay; he and Cink were sturdy teammates in the Nike camp, but as a student of golf history, he knew full well what he had watched unfold through these past four days.

As Watson climbed to the top on his own, Oxman, carrying the large black-and-white bag with "Adams Golf" stitched neatly across the side, had to be literally pushed up the hill. Cink 2-putted for par. Watson, now grinding, settled over his 8-footer and calmly rattled the ball into the hole.

Now, an 8-footer falls!

After two holes, Cink remained a shot ahead.

The strange traveling circus shifted to the par-5 17th hole. Gallery, players, caddies, officials, reporters, television cameras all in one neat little migratory package. Cink and Watson and their caddies arrived in separate golf carts. It had the feel of the last singles match with the Ryder Cup hanging in the balance. Rarely, if ever, do so many players return to the field of action just to observe.

All gathered, at this point, to witness the final unraveling of Old Tom Watson.

"He was tired," said Neil Oxman with a hint of disheartenment.

"The key thing in the playoff is to hit good shots," says Watson. "I hit maybe one good shot and Stewart Cink hardly missed a shot. He hit every shot like he was supposed to, and I didn't hit a single shot like I wanted. My second shot on 5 was fat, my tee shot on 6 was a block, my tee ball at 17 was the killer. I tried to hit it real hard and hit a draw. Every once in a while, I'll hit a hook like that. It doesn't come often, but it sure came at the wrong time."

"I was hoping he would gather himself," said Watson's old friend Jack Nicklaus. "But it was quite obvious in the extra holes, Tom was spent. I don't think he was tired. He's very fit, so I don't think he would get tired in that situation. But emotionally, he was spent. All his emotions were spent in those first eighteen holes. When Stewart made birdie at 18 and Tom made bogey, it goes right through you.

"You try to come back and grab for more energy, but . . ."

"Aw, that's no excuse," Watson says quickly. "People are looking for excuses for how badly I played out there. That series of shots just weren't there. No excuse at all."

When your legs don't work, as Oxman suggested, the ball can go and hide quickly. And his tee shot on the third extra hole did just that, quickly snapping left into the thickest rough on the golf course. In fact, it took several minutes just to find the ball, and once they did, Watson wasn't sure he could do much with it. While Cink was comfortably in the lead and near the fairway, Watson could only shake his head.

"I don't know if I can get it out of here, Ox, but I'm gonna give it a try," Watson said before chopping a bale of hay with his wedge and seeing the ball squirt low and left, still deep and ugly.

Cink meantime reached the par-5 green in 2 and while Watson was penciling a dead-tired double bogey on his scorecard, Cink was 2-putting for birdie. Just like that, Watson was 4 shots down with one hole to play.

"I was in the fairway on 17," recalls Cink, "and had about 250 yards left. There is danger on that second shot. With a 4-iron and a wind howling, I could have fallen a little short and ended up in a bunker 30 yards away. That would not have been a good place to be. But once I hit it on the green and cozied it up for birdie, I knew I had won it.

"I remember just thinking, 'This is really sweet.'"

As the engraver was carefully etching "Stewart Cink" on the Claret Jug, Watson was putting the finishing touches on one of the most excruciating letdowns in sports history. He missed the 18th fairway and green for the first time all week and carded his second straight bogey there.

Cink played his second shot on 18 reminiscent of the 7-iron shot that Watson had hit there thirty-two years before, winding up just 2 feet from the pin. And like Watson then with Nicklaus, Cink made birdie to close out the stunning reversal of fortunes.

It was his second birdie in an hour at 18, and he won the playoff by 6 shots, the largest margin of victory since the Open reduced the playoff to four holes. It was, however, far from an Open playoff record. The great South African Bobby Locke beat Harry Bradshaw by a dozen strokes in a thirty-six-hole playoff at Sandwich in 1949.

No matter. It could have been just one shot and it would have stung Watson just as deeply.

As Watson tapped in his bogey putt on the final hole, ABC's host, Mike Tirico, put the planet's emotions into words: "Thank you, Tom Watson. We will never forget this."

In the twilight of a magnificent Scottish Sunday, at approximately 7:30, Stewart Cink was proclaimed "the champion golfer of the year" and Tom Watson was a fifty-nine-year-old second.

After he shook hands with the victorious Cink, Watson turned to his old friend Neil Oxman.

"I didn't get silly or anything," said Oxman, "but I put my arm around him and told him, 'You are just amazing.' I was so proud of him."

"Tom played beautifully all week. He handled himself well the entire time," said Nicklaus later. "He showed a lotta class. I know he's not happy, but he should be so pleased about his performance."

After hugging Hilary and consoling a distraught son Michael on the phone, Watson tried desperately to bring a lightness to this seeming tragedy.

"The old fogey almost did it," he laughed. "Woulda made for a great story. It just wasn't to be."

And then he looked out at the crowd gathered almost as much to pay their respects as to hear his closing words.

"Hey, this ain't a funeral here," he said with a smile.

But inside, and not so very deep at all, the turmoil raged as the reality of what he had done began to set in.

"I may never have the chance again to beat the kids," he

admitted, "but I take one thing from that last hole in regulation: Hitting both the tee shot and the approach exactly the
way I meant to . . . wasn't good enough. I had to finish.

"It's an extreme disappointment. In my profession, when
you have the chance to win the World Open, as I call it, and
give it away, it is very disappointing.

"I now remember what it was like to play against the
kids. Coming here, I dreamed that I could win because of
how I was playing and the fact that I know how to play this
course. That dream almost came true. I am so glad it all
happened."

Months later, it still burned at his insides.

"Sure, it hurts to have it in your grasp," he said, recalling
the pain. "I told Hilary that right after. She knew exactly
what I meant. It was good to have her there to control that.
But it still hurts."

Cink cradled the Claret Jug and tried to sum up his immediate emotions, a nearly impossible task.

"Extraordinary is just the tip of the iceberg," he said.
"Not only was I playing on one of my favorite courses, in a
wonderful tournament, but I was playing against Tom Watson.
I mean, this sorta thing just doesn't happen. I grew up watching Tom Watson on television, hoping that one day I could
follow in his footsteps. He turned back the clock here. I just
feel so fortunate to have been a part of it."

I grew up watching Tom Watson on television.

How many men in the initial field of 156 would say that
at one point or another as the 138th Open marched dramati-

cally toward Sunday? Some were so young they hardly knew who Tom Watson was. In the end, however, everyone knew.

In a way, it could have been what Tom Watson had said in another era about Jack Nicklaus. When Watson turned professional in 1971, Nicklaus had already won eight of his eighteen major championships. The television set might have been smaller, and black-and-white, but surely the young redhead from Kansas had carefully studied every Nicklaus move. To compete against him? Imagine the thought. And to that end, sit in Stewart Cink's chair late on a Sunday evening in July 2009 and allow yourself a brief perusal of the names along the Claret Jug's bottom band. You had to go back twenty-six summers, but there, for the fifth time, was the man you just defeated.

Shudder if you will. Stewart Cink did.

23

"A WRINKLE IN TIME"

In the minutes and hours following the four-hole play-off, when lives changed forever, when Watson's will no longer could force the issue and Stewart Cink walked away with the coveted Claret Jug, the scene resembled precisely what Watson had joked about—a funeral of sorts.

Though most were happy for Cink—a pleasant and honest young man who had paid enormous dues over the years—they still felt they had watched the unraveling of history. Unashamed, they cried and both Watson and Oxman spent much of their time, in the words of one onlooker, "comforting the mourners."

Oxman knew how they felt.

"Emotions aren't intellectual," he said later. "An international superstar came up to me, gave me a really prolonged hug, and I could feel he was crying. He walked away, spent a couple minutes composing himself, and then returned with tears still in his eyes."

A man had won a golf tournament. Another had lost. It

happens almost every Sunday of the year somewhere in the world. And yet rarely, if ever, do the results elicit this tremendous outpouring of care and sympathy.

Even in the media center, where dozens of writers tried to assemble their thoughts, there was a tinge of sorrow.

"I knew we weren't good enough to deserve writing a Watson win," mourned one old columnist. Bitter that they had been deprived of the honor, some took it out on Cink.

Cink, unfairly, was seen by the *Financial Times of London* as "the man who shot Santa Claus."

"Like the giant ogre in a children's scare story," wrote Mark Reason in the *Telegraph* that evening, "Cink stomped all over this Open Championship and crushed our dreams."

The big man dressed that Sunday in vivid green took it all with the grace of a champion, all the while knowing that he had done only what he was set out to do.

"I don't feel ashamed," he said about ruining a good story. "In the end, it's a tournament to see who lasts the longest. I surely don't feel disappointed. I'm pleased as Punch. I'm also proud of the way Tom Watson played. Not only did he show how great a golfer he is, but he showed what a great game we all play, the longevity that can exist.

"We thought Jack Nicklaus hung the moon when he won the Masters at forty-six. This is thirteen years on from that, thirteen more years of age. It just says a lot about golf."

His tweets now came fast and furious, one after another as he shared his joy with hundreds of thousands of followers. He attached photos in most tweets of someone pouring

Guinness into the Claret Jug, of the jug sitting on the breakfast table next to the cereal, of the jug in its aluminum case being placed in the overhead space on the Cink family's flight home to Atlanta.

The Claret Jug is precisely what its name implies, a replica of a jug used to serve claret wine. The first eleven Open winners received a wide red Morrocan-leather belt studded with silver buckles and emblems. The rule in those days was that any man who won what they called "the Challenge Belt" three years in a row could keep it forever. Young Tom Morris finished off that task in 1870, and so the R&A went in search of a new gift for the victor.

After several years of serious decision making, they came up with the Claret Jug in 1873. The original has been kept every year since in a special case in the R&A clubhouse at St Andrews. The winner gets a replica and can keep it for as long as he is the reigning Open champion. There are three deep bands along the bottom of the trophy on which the winner, year, and site of each championship is carefully hand-engraved.

"We were standing there at 18 waiting for the awards presentation," Cink recalls with a large smile, "and I had the jug in my hand. I remember saying to Tom, 'I can't believe your name is on here five times and mine is only on here once.

"'But at least it's the most recent.'"

Watson smiled through clenched teeth, appreciating the attempt at humor. He looked to his left as they gathered for the presentation ceremony and there stood his running mate through the first two rounds, the sixteen-year-old Italian phenom Matteo Manassero, who would receive the silver medal as low amateur.

Watson put an arm around the slim young man's shoulders. "You'll be here one day." He nodded toward the Claret Jug. "One day, you will be here holding that."

Manassero, who had worked as hard on his English as he had on his golf game, needed no translation. He beamed with delight.

————

There are eleven roundabouts on the road from Turnberry to the major expressway that is the M6 going south to London. It is a journey of just a fraction over four hundred miles and, once aboard the major artery, hopelessly boring.

Neil Oxman sat comfortably behind the right-hand-steering wheel of his rental car and pointed it ultimately toward a village on the outskirts of London called Bagshot, which dates back to before the 1300s, toward a quaint little hotel called Pennyhill Park Hotel and Spa. Once again, hardly the usual bunking spot for tour caddies. Located on 123 acres of rolling parkland, it has played host to such luminaries as Russell Crowe and Nicole Kidman, though reportedly not at the same time.

Oxman, like his boss Tom Watson, is a man of taste.

With BBC radio for background noise and the roundabouts to keep his attention, the bespectacled caddie had a solid eight hours to digest what had just happened.

———

Watson, who had just given back the 138th Open, remained behind at the luxurious Turnberry Hotel in a suite with his name on the door. While Oxman could not afford the desire that night to sleep on his drive south, Watson tried to in bed and failed miserably.

Between trying to come to terms with his emotions while settling the tearful response around him, he tossed and turned the entire night.

He received so many e-mails of congratulations and condolence that his laptop once again gave up in anger. His cell phone crashed as well, as it had earlier in the weekend. It was his only way of knowing just how much his four days in July had deeply affected the world. So isolated at Turnberry and so insulated from the rest of the planet, he knew that he had been on the heels of something very special, he said so several times. But he didn't realize just *how* special until his methods of communication exploded. Friends, competitors, people who had watched in frustrated sorrow, desperately wanted to let him know how they felt.

"I've been overwhelmed," said Watson, "and humbled by the reaction of people. It's been a very disappointing time but also very special for me. Who would think that losing a golf tournament would be that special?

"I didn't sleep much that Sunday night, but to let something like that linger on and change your outlook on life, no."

Of all the messages that made it through, several had enormous impact on the man. One was from his old friend and rival Jack Nicklaus. It was the first text message Nicklaus had ever sent in his life, though his wife had sent Watson several throughout the weekend, urging him on.

"On Sunday night," recalled Watson, "Jack wrote that he never watched someone play eighteen holes on TV, never before, but that he had watched this one from hole 1 to hole 18. And he said on 18, 'You hit two perfect shots and the ball should have stayed at the back of the green and it didn't. You hit the right putter for your third shot and you just didn't make the putt. You couldn't have done it any differently.'

"When the greatest player in history pats you on the shoulder and says you did the right thing, well, he wasn't patronizing me, he was being realistic. It was much appreciated."

The second message was as devastating as Nicklaus's was uplifting. Watson learned that an old friend had died of brain cancer.

"He was just a couple years older than me," said Watson. "It put what happened on Sunday back into the proper perspective."

A third message came from a young soldier named Leroy Petry, a staff sergeant in the Army Rangers who lost his hand in a grenade explosion as he saved the lives of comrades in Afghanistan. Up for the Congressional Medal of Honor, Petry was one of many Wounded Warriors met by Watson and other golfers on tours of hospitals and battle-fields worldwide over the last few years.

"These people I met at Walter Reed and Bethesda hospital and all over Iraq," said Watson, "many have contacted me and said, 'Congratulations and, oh, by the way, when you're in a neck-high bunker or you have a 4-footer, just remember, it's just a game.'

"I give them credit for keeping me on the straight and level here and not getting too disappointed. That's perspective."

———

As Oxman drove and Watson tossed and turned, newspaper editors across the planet tried to summarize the entire episode in a few choice words:

"A Wrinkle in Time."

"Brilliant, my dear Watson."

"British Open: Oh, well."

"One Putt from a Miracle."

"Topsy Turnberry."

"One Man's Pleasure . . ."

If they weren't allowed the luxury of documenting history, they could at least compete for cleverest headline.

"Watson once was known as the biggest choker of them all," wrote Mark Reason in the *Telegraph*, referring to times long past when Watson's putter failed him at the worst of moments. "On Sunday, he handed off that title to every spectator in the grandstand. We fought back the tears like mourners at a funeral. But what a ride Tom took us all on.

"Cink is the champion golfer of the year, but Watson is the champion man."

———

While Watson fought sleep, occasionally rising to peek out the window, catching a haunting glimpse in the early morning haze of the large rock off the coast, Oxman set his cruise control and pointed the car south, his mind racing. Renaissance man that he is, he allowed himself to switch hats for a moment and review the past four days as he would a movie for NPR.

"With a great book or a great movie, you know someone has already written the end," he said. "If you're idiot enough, you skip to the last chapter of the book. With the movie, you can often foresee the end and, anyway, you know the director knows, the scripter knows.

"But as we were standing there on the 18th fairway on Sunday evening, Tom had hit his last shot into the green, he had the Claret Jug almost in his hands . . . but we still didn't know how it would end. No one knew. The script hadn't been written. That's why it was so amazing.

"The actual ending we got would've made a better movie. While I'm disappointed for Tom, I really am, more than that I'm unbelievably proud of him. I was there for the overture, never more than a few feet away during the entire performance. And I was there for the epilogue. If he had won the tournament, I couldn't have been more proud."

————

As Cink's name was being carefully etched on the silver band at the bottom of the Claret Jug, the staff of the Turnberry Hotel was busy with another important task. Almost before the k was inscribed, they had gone into the Cinks' room, removed all of their clothing and luggage, and moved them into the latest of the champions' suites.

At the Turnberry Hotel, the suites are, like everything else, very understated. The polished brass plaques on the doors simply offer the champion's last name. The suite labeled "Watson" is appropriately a study in gray. Teal walls above gray wainscoting frame the living room. A white fireplace faces a gray bookcase with comfortable sofas and chairs in between. There are a few original works of art on the walls but nothing to indicate to the unsuspecting just who this "Watson" was and why he deserved a door with his name on it. Until the hotel was refurbished in 2009, the great advantage of being a champion was not the size of the suite but the air-conditioning, something the rest of the elegant old hotel never had.

The going rate for such a suite is £700 to £800 a night, well over $1,000 American, but the hotel does not advertise "Stay in the Champion's Suite," instead simply offering four elegant ocean-view suites.

"They had moved everything," says a still-astonished

Cink, "even the toothbrushes, into that suite. Unbelievable, and it had air-conditioning! You know I'm just as happy at a Hampton Inn as I am at Ritz-Carlton, but to have this room with my name on the front was really awesome. That was the coolest thing that has ever happened to me after a win."

"Saturday when Tom had the lead," remembers Chris Card, the new director of golf at Turnberry, "we actually had a serious discussion about what we would do about the suite if he won. Would we have two Tom Watson suites? We figured maybe we would have a Watson '77 and a Watson '09. Turns out, we have a Stewart Cink suite, and that's just great with us."

Cink's Sunday evening was a blur. After meeting with the media, he was whisked to a room upstairs in the clubhouse where he met with eighteen members of the R&A and the Turnberry organizing committee. There he talked fondly of the experience of battling Tom Watson, one of his heroes.

"He seemed to want to talk more about Tom than himself," said Chris Card. "He just couldn't find enough words to define the experience. It was great listening to him."

When he was finished there, Cink cradled the Claret Jug in his arms and walked across the street, climbing the ninety-nine steps by himself to the hotel. The lobby was packed with fans and when they spotted the newly crowned champion, they burst into wondrous applause. People having dinner in the three restaurants off the lobby left their meals and joined the celebration.

An hour later, as he and Lisa had dinner by themselves, one fan after another approached the table and asked for a picture.

"I hate to bother you," was the usual prompt.

"Hey, you don't win this jug every day," was Cink's smiling response. "It's as much yours as mine."

And as his dinner grew cold, he posed for picture after picture, a major champion at long last.

———

Meanwhile a half mile down the road from Turnberry, Watson and his wife and a good friend named Tuck Clagett, who grew up with Watson in Kansas City and had flown in specifically to help celebrate what he expected to be history, had dinner at a popular restaurant called Wildings.

"It was quite an experience," recalls Watson. "I didn't expect what happened, but we walked into the restaurant and everybody stood up and clapped. We had eaten there four other times that week and the same thing had happened, but it was louder Sunday night.

"We had a nice dinner, and afterward there came this line of people asking for an autograph or a picture. We must have stayed another hour doing that.

"We went back to the room and I guess I got about an hour of sleep thinking about what had happened that day. The adrenaline kept me awake."

"After everything died down," recalls Cink, "Lisa and I

ran into Tom and Hilary on the stairs of the hotel. Musta been close to midnight. I had the Claret Jug in the case and we stopped and talked.

"Tom told this story about how he had taken it on a fishing trip to Canada and it got damaged. How the boys he was with had a good time with it.

"It was cool. To hear that story from the guy you just beat in a playoff. It was so cool that he and I could go from being ultimate competitors to being two guys sharing stories on the steps, from doing battle to telling tales.

"I think it says a lot about the game and the man."

———

Oxman drove on, the babble of the radio just white noise. He broke down the week into parts. The opening-round 65 was his man's finest start at the Open in his long and storied history. The second round began so poorly, with bogeys scattered through the first six holes, and ended so brilliantly with that 60-foot birdie putt on the final hole. Oh, if he could have shaved that to 52 feet and left the remaining 8 good for Sunday.

The weekend was a blur until it came to a screeching, mind-numbing halt on the other side of the seventy-second hole.

"Looking back," he said, "the most remarkable thing was . . . we were out early on Thursday, 8:09 tee time. Tom birdied the first hole, and you know there is a leaderboard at every hole. He never once left that leaderboard for seventy-two holes. Even with that bad stretch on Friday. I mean, it doesn't happen like that. Hell, it doesn't happen like that at the Quad Cities Open.

"This wasn't some guy catching fire on his back nine on Sunday. This was a guy a few weeks shy of sixty facing the enormous pressure for four full days and he never once wavered.

"My first thought when it was all over was a question: How many more times can this happen to this man before he's too old?"

As Oxman was lost in his own thoughts that Sunday night, Watson rubbed his eyes one more time in a fruitless attempt at sleep.

"It was fun having the kids who were *my* kids' age out there just looking up to you, saying, 'What are you doing out here doing this?' and then saying, 'All right, nice going, you still can play.'

"When it's all said and done, one of the things I hope that will come out of my life is that my peers will say, 'You know, that Watson, he was a helluva golfer.'"

He would not have to wait. The accolades poured in, despite his finish.

"It's remarkable what he did," said Chip Beck. "He wasn't really concerned with how he was doing, and that's the mark of a good champion who enjoyed where he was, didn't get tied up in the things you and I do.

"If I can play that good when I am sixty, I will be very happy."

"He's the best wind player I've ever seen," said Jim Colbert. "Best in my forty-four years out here. So I wasn't at all surprised at what he did. First of all, he's a great player and he doesn't say he can win when he can't. He's not an idle talker."

"He's probably a better ball striker now than when he was in his prime," said Fred Funk. "He was talking all week about the magic of the place and the spirituality, and he has a comfort level with that golf course that's unprecedented. So it didn't surprise me at all. Nerves didn't beat him, just bad luck."

"It would have been a great thing if he had won the tournament," said Billy Casper, "but it was still a phenomenal exhibition of playing."

"I don't think anyone has ever played links golf like him, ever," said Nick Price. "And as an American, well, it's just astonishing. His passion and love for that game is so evident. To do what he did, the course so much longer and the nerves aren't like when they were in the twenties and thirties. To have that control, wow, just amazing."

Former PGA champion Lanny Wadkins took his praise to another level.

"If the PGA Tour slogan is 'These guys are good,' well, maybe the Champions Tour slogan should be 'These guys are great.'

"I'm sorry, but that generation oughta be embarrassed. Old men kicking their butts two years in a row. Outside of Tiger and Phil [Mickelson], it's a generation without imagination."

"Someone asked me what Tom would take away from this," said Jack Nicklaus. "My guess is it's the same thing I took away from 1977. When people ask me what I remember most about our duel, I tell them I remember I lost. Knowing Tom, I think he will say the same thing.

"This was absolutely Tom Watson's Open to win or lose. But he long ago secured his legacy in the game. This would just have been something to add to the top of the cake."

24

WHO WAS WATCHING?

Because the world seemed to want to put an arm around Tom Watson and comfort him, because the world supposedly cried at the outcome, because I was there and a part of the entire adventure, I became so wrapped up in the historical significance that I and a thousand more just like me lost our sense of what those four days in July really meant. It turned out, to most except us, very little if you believe in raw numbers.

The overnight television ratings for Sunday's telecast were a meager 3.9, which means that 96 percent of U.S. viewers did not tune in.

When those numbers became evident in the hours following the championship, there seemed to be a collective "huh?" Here was the most astonishing story in years, perhaps ever, in golf, a story that did not catch anyone by surprise as it was building. It began on Thursday and allowed the television audience more than enough time to decide it was special enough to watch.

If Tiger Woods had been in the mix, those numbers would have escalated dramatically. He appeared to be the only athlete who had the ability to shift TV audiences by double and sometimes triple digits. But he was long gone, having missed the cut.

"The U.S. sporting public," wrote Christine Brennan in *USA Today*, "was presented with a choice last weekend that it doesn't often face. It was given the most compelling sports story of the year, but one that didn't involve a household sports name for anyone under 35. To follow that story, fans had to watch a golf tournament without the sports world's leading personality. And, by and large, they chose not to do that."

Golf is a peripheral sport on the television scene. Its numbers are rarely anything close to what football or baseball draws unless, of course, Tiger is in the action. The Open also presents a unique scheduling problem in that it comes on in America during the midmorning and finishes shortly after lunchtime. Deliver that on a Sunday in July when a good many fans are either in church or on the golf course themselves, and the audience pool becomes severely limited.

Though the numbers for the 2009 Open were very similar to most Opens over the years, Watson's excitement did generate a definite increase in Champions Tour television ratings for the remainder of the season. And it began the following week at the Senior British Open when ABC's final-round coverage gathered an impressive 25 percent increase in ratings over the previous season, despite Watson's middling finish.

Watson climbed dramatically not only in the eyes of the

interested world but in the official world rankings as well. He began those four days in July almost even with the book-makers' odds, 1,374th in the entire golf world. At the end of the playoff on Sunday evening, he had climbed to 105th, the largest one-week leap since they began ranking players in 1986. Had he won, he would have jumped to 45th, a spot that would have automatically earned him eligibility as part of the top fifty for various Tour and World Golf Champion-ship tournaments.

Stewart Cink moved up from thirty-third to ninth.

25

TAKE REFUGE
IN ROUTINE

Watson and Hilary flew to London the following morning to join Oxman in preparation for the following week's Senior British Open at the lovely old parkland course known as Sunningdale Golf Club. The short flight was interrupted constantly by fans bringing items to Watson to sign, many handing him that morning's tabloid with the huge headline "Cruel in the Sun." He signed them all with a benevolent, patient smile.

It was a great solace, that scheduling. If he had had a week or two off following the Open, it might have been a wound too deep to heal. Instead, fresh challenges immediately awaited.

"It helped take my mind off the previous week," Watson says, "and allowed me to start concentrating on that week."

It is four days later now, four days and five hundred and fifty miles south, as Tom Watson walks onto the practice green at Sunningdale, thirty miles west of London, and drops two Titleist Pro V1s at his feet. The putter, a wicked-looking Odyssey with sharp wings protruding from the back, is the same one he used so dramatically seventy-one holes the week before. It is also the one that was in his grip on the seventy-second when his hands suddenly became nearly sixty years old again.

It is the opening day of the Senior British Open, and the remnants of one of golf's most resounding weeks ever still hang like an electric storm over Sunningdale. Every man, from player to official to fan, still talks of what might have been.

"I cried," said Gary Player. "My wife cried, my daughter back home in South Africa cried. We all cried."

"It was still the greatest week in my golf memory," said Jay Haas. "What a story it would have been, huh?"

"I was thinking I might pass on a practice round that Monday," said Watson. "But I needed to go out and play and get on with my life just like I always have. Surprisingly, I wasn't too tired because that adrenaline was still with me from the week before. A good practice round, a good dinner, a good sleep and I would be good as new again. But that Monday, the magnitude of the response of people really started to sink in. People said how much they enjoyed it, how they were pulling for me, how disappointed they were that I didn't win."

He would find great solace at this beautiful old creation, as have so many over the decades. Bobby Jones played what has been called the "perfect round" there in 1926 as he qualified for the Open Championship: 33 going out and another 33 coming home, 33 shots and 33 putts. He loved it so much that he told friends he wanted to take it all home with him and, in a sense, he did. He took bits and pieces of what he found at Sunningdale and used them when he built Augusta National.

Tom Watson's solace, however, took a while to settle in, three-quarters of a century later. Teeth clenched, he stood over the first ball on the practice green that Thursday. His Pro V1 is marked very carefully, because so many on the tour play a similar ball. Watson and Oxman use a black Sharpie to fill in one dimple above the *T* in Titleist on each side of the golf ball.

The hole was 8 feet away. "This . . . for the Open Championship," we used to whisper as children, and I imagined a similar thought running through his mind that day.

The first practice putt missed, and then the second. It got worse. You could see his hands turning white, the grip so tight. He mumbled something to himself and moved on to another distance, his tee time minutes away. He was paired again with Greg Norman.

For nearly seventy-one subsequent holes of the Senior Championship, that same putter continued to fail him. Putts of every length slid past, stayed short, fell left or right. Finally, on the seventy-second hole of a tournament he would not win, he stood over an 8-foot putt for birdie. It meant very little in the grand scheme of things, but meant more than any of us will ever know to Old Tom Watson.

He took his time, measured his distance, stroked it firmly, and watched it disappear. An ironic smile crept across his golden face as he acknowledged the knowing, loving gallery.

"Oh, what he would have given for that stroke a week ago," mourned a commentator on Sky TV, which was carrying the tournament live in the United Kingdom.

It was, in the end, the very essence of the game another Old Tom helped draw up two centuries ago. You never, ever, conquer it. You simply make friends and treat it kindly and hope one day it returns the favor.

———

The following months were overwhelming for Thomas Sturges Watson.

"It's been pretty amazing," he told me in a lengthy interview some months later. "I've had a lotta people come up to me and say they watched the British Open this summer. They were there, or they got their kids to watch. I think that's the biggest thing. The parents and people from all walks of life were watching it, people who don't ever watch golf. People told me they don't like golf but they had to watch it.

"My age made it unique. That was it. Can this old has-been do something that's never been done before?"

He played the equivalent of four straight major championships in the late stages of the 2009 summer, from the

Open to the Senior British, on to the U.S. Senior Open and finally the Jeld-Wen Championship, until, exhausted, he and Hilary sought shelter in the shadow of his birthplace. On a four-hundred-acre plot of land near Stillwater, Kansas, just south of Kansas City, he was able to recharge his aging batteries.

While the golf world continued to murmur at the mere audacity of his performance at Turnberry, Watson and his wife took refuge in the place they simply call "the Ranch," which he has owned for more than a quarter century. With rolling pastures and ponds filled with bass, it is a bastion of privacy rarely invaded by anyone other than the closest friends.

Andy North, the two-time U.S. Open champion and one of Watson's oldest and dearest friends, is one.

"He just loves that place," North told Dick Mudry for a piece in the Outback Steakhouse Pro-Am program titled *Greens and Acres*. "Deep down, he's a Midwestern kid. He likes to work on the farm. He doesn't mind getting dirty and loves to hunt and fish. He can go out and do something and at the end of the day, he feels like he's accomplished something. It's rewarding for him to get on a tractor and turn off the world."

Golf is rarely far from Watson's thoughts, no matter where he rests. The Ranch has a practice facility where he tunes up his game.

In the time following the Open and all of its attendant hoopla, however, the Ranch was more like Superman's Secret Citadel, a place of escape and rejuvenation, a real Fortress of Solitude.

254

Jim Huber

"He's got a tractor," Hilary told Mudry, "and mows the grass. In the fall we [harvest] prairie grass. There's a huge vegetable garden and roses. He's very busy when we are there. But when we get there, we're in another world. It's our refuge."

———

Just what kind of impact did Tom Watson's four days in July have on the Champions Tour? There are some who claim it can be measured in both acclaim and dollars and cents.

"He came out of Turnberry as a rock star," says Tour director of communications Michael McPhillips. "And we have seen a direct response in terms of sponsorship and backing."

Indeed, while both the PGA and LPGA tours saw cutbacks, the 2010 Champions Tour actually added tournaments, bringing its total to twenty-six, and increased prize money to a record average of $1.98 million per tournament.

And that Hickory, North Carolina, event, which seemed in such dire straits? It returned to that schedule to great sighs of relief, underwritten by a new title sponsor. For at least the following year, it would be known as the Ensure Classic at Rock Barn, brought to you by the vitamin- and mineral-enriched health shake. There seemed to be no direct regional tie-in, simply an opening filled, a logical connection to the senior crowd made.

———

The wonderfully-named racehorse named Whaston, which seemed to set the tone for an improbable week in July, ran twice more over hurdles in 2009, finished second both times, and was sold. Since there is no senior tour for Thorough-breds, it is likely he will spend the remainder of his years manicuring a British pasture without the slightest clue of his serendipitous turn.

———

Jeremy Kavanagh, the journeyman golfer who rode Whaston to Watson in the space of twenty-four Turnberry hours, re-turned to the golf's hinterlands, once again giving the South African Tour a try. His experience in Scotland gave rise to a personal Web site but failed to elevate his game.

"Life is too short not to pursue your dreams" is the headline above a large photograph on his site from the first round of the Open, and there stands one of the large yellow scoreboards. Tom Watson's name is at the very top, his opening-round 65 finished. Kavanagh's name is at the bot-tom, 3 under par after seven holes.

In the foreground of the lone picture on the site with the wispy rough nipping at his knees, Kavanagh himself is mak-ing his way to the 8th green. Those dreams would soon come crashing down as he wound up shooting a first-round 74, 9 shots more than his hero.

2 6

ORDER THE SENIOR SPECIAL

It is altogether appropriate that Tom Watson would spend his sixtieth birthday playing in the shadow of one of the greatest moments of his professional career. Not in Scotland, not in an Open, but along the Monterey Peninsula in California, just a mile or so from the spot where he so magically chipped in at the 17th hole of Pebble Beach to upset Nicklaus and win the 1982 U.S. Open.

Now twenty-seven years and three months later, September 4, 2009, and the first round of a Champions Tour event is shared with youngsters, benefiting the First Tee program. Youngsters who were now looking at the man with not only newfound respect but actual knowledge, for a change.

"Used to be," Watson says, laughing, "there were blank stares and 'Who is this old guy?' Now, it's big smiles, saying 'Yeah, saw you in the British Open'."

Much, of course, was made that day at Del Monte, the

course that shares the tournament with Pebble Beach, of the Birthday Boy. Someone suggested it would be altogether appropriate that he go out and shoot 60. But Watson had a better idea.

"It'll be fun to go into these restaurants like Denny's and just look 'em in the eye and say, 'You know, I need the Senior Special menu today.'

"Thing is, you don't get as much food but you get it quite a bit cheaper. Of course, I don't need as much food these days, anyway."

He gave thought to still playing the game professionally at the age of sixty.

"When I was forty," he told reporters, "I said I wouldn't ever play after fifty. Well, here I am. I'm lucky, not a question. It's hard not to go out there and get the excitement of teeing it up in competition. That's what keeps me going, the thrill of still putting it all on the line."

———

Nearly two months later, Watson received more tangible results from his run at Turnberry. The Royal and Ancient, golf's governing body that had dictated sixty years of age as the official finish line for the Open Championship, changed its mind. "Our intention was never to remove players still at the top of their game from competing in the Open," said R&A chief executive Peter Dawson.

Having seen first Greg Norman at Birkdale and now Tom Watson at Turnberry do precisely that, the R&A voted to amend the rule so that former champions who finish in the top ten in the previous five Opens get a five-year exemption.

"We have introduced this exemption as a direct response to seeing two of our great Open champions, both in their fifties, challenging to win our championship."

———

Stewart Cink tried his best not to be lost in the lingering aftershock of Turnberry.

Rarely, if ever, has the world been given such intimate access to a champion's glory, and it didn't stop a day or two after the victory. He took the Claret Jug to restaurants and hockey practices and radio stations. He nearly took it one too many places.

During the week of the Tour Championship two months later at East Lake Golf Club in Atlanta, Cink had the jug safely locked in its aluminum case but sitting inside his open locker in the clubhouse. He returned that afternoon to find it missing. Padraig Harrington, familiar with the case and its contents from his two years of ownership prior to Cink, had carefully lifted it and placed it in his own locker.

For fun.

It lasted only until someone whispered to Cink what had happened.

Cink laughed. "Hey, he had it for two years, I've only had it for two months. If he wants it that bad, I'll let him borrow it."

27

A FIELD OF DREAMS

It is August 2009 and absolutely pristine along the Ayrshire coast. With temperatures in the mid-seventies under crystal clear skies, it is the kind of weather the local chamber of commerce can only dream of.

"Feels like the Carolinas," said Chris Card, who had left those parts in June to become Turnberry's Director of Golf. "Isn't it supposed to be rainy and blustery here?"

Tourists, mostly Americans, have flocked to Turnberry's gate in huge numbers since the Open, eager to experience the course where Watson nearly made history.

Oddly enough, despite the fact that the Open was long gone, the huge grandstands encircling the 18th green remained and wouldn't be taken down until late September. The thrill of playing any of the Open rotation in the days and weeks following the championship is magnified greatly by the remaining empty grandstands, as if a yawning confirmation. Yes, it was here. This is what Tom Watson saw as he stared down that 8-iron last month. If I close my eyes, I can hear the enormous gallery giving the ball directions. Stop, here, please stop, no!

And to a man and woman, at the end of their round, no matter where they happen to finish, they go to the exact spot behind the final green, drop a ball in the thick green rough, and test their own resolve. Card watches them from his office in the clubhouse nearby and smiles, wondering if yet another plaque must be placed in the grounds of this old gem of a golf course.

"It was here . . ."

The vacationing golfers stare at the mound leading up to the green, assess their chances, wonder if a wedge might have been the better choice back in July, and slowly discover it was neither the putter nor the wedge but the pure imagination of the man at work that evening.

In the quiet of the moment, a whisper comes on the freshening wind.

"The old fogey almost did it. The dream almost came true."

EPILOGUE

The veal was tough and the sauce watery. Strange what one remembers when the conversation is just as unmanageable. The tiny Italian restaurant around the corner from Columbus Circle in Manhattan was so crowded that night in the mid-1990s that the couples on either side seemed to be hanging over our table, listening to what my agent had to say.

"This is hard for me," he started, fiddling with long strands of spaghetti. I suspected he knew it was just as hard for me. "I know you're happy at CNN, but I think you could do much better elsewhere."

At that point, I had been with CNN for more than a dozen years, having moved there in its second year of existence, and I *was* happy. Though I had been removed from the anchor desk, which always seemed to be the glamour position, I was balancing my time between covering golf and creating a regular show called *The Sporting Life with Jim Huber*. Presumptuous, but it was their idea to include the name, not mine.

"So . . ." my (now ex) agent continued, "wow, this is . . . I've never asked any of my clients this . . . have you ever considered, um, coloring your hair?"

The instant flush, like a full-faced mask, turned me warm red. I felt the entire restaurant raise its collective head and chuckle.

"Why in the world . . . ?" I stammered. My hair, what was left of it, had stumbled from a dishwater brown to a late-winter gray in recent years, but no one had said much about it.

"Well," he said, "it all has to do with age and the public's perception. I keep running into roadblocks, executives saying, 'Oh, well, we like his work, but he's a bit old for us.' I thought maybe if you just got rid of the gray, it might help."

Why should my age be a detriment? Didn't it make more sense to hire a seasoned performer rather than someone who had gray roots once a month? And why did I care, since my current employer seemed adequately pleased with my work?

I thought of that dinner once or twice during Tom Watson's stunning four days in July of 2009. It had nothing to do with hair color or jaw firmness but rather with that one word—perception.

If we had not been handed a calendar or his résumé, if he had simply been a golfer of average height and weight, if we had not counted the wrinkles or age spots, if indeed he had been just one of the 156 men gathered to take on Turnberry, would we have been just as flabbergasted at his performance?

Of course not. It is, sadly, how we are judged at times. *Not bad for an old guy.*

I recall sitting next to him in our interview cabin, silently awaiting my cue, watching him out of the corner of my eye, calculating.

Here was a man just barely my junior. When he began his professional career in 1971, I was beginning my own career roller-coaster ride. When he won his first PGA tournament in 1974, I was in the throes of leaving the newspaper business for what surely would be a long and successful career in radio.

When he won the memorable Open at Turnberry in 1977, I was leaving radio for local television that very same week. And when I was exiting Atlanta's WXIA-TV for the fledgling CNN in July 1984, Tom Watson was coming to the end of one of the most remarkable stretches in Open history, having won three and finishing second once in the first five championships of the '80s.

Now here we sat in our own field of quiet. I wondered about the vagaries of the Champions Tour, whether a man goes there feeling old or feeling rejuvenated. There is no senior circuit for sportswriters and broadcasters. We scribble and talk until our own special brand of yips takes over and we either leave on our own or dye our hair and go out faking it.

Like Watson, experience becomes our chief ally. We have been here before, seen these same treacherous hills and valleys, learned how to handle them. We still stumble, we still ask

stupid questions, we still paint ourselves into impossible corners, we are hardly immune to humanity.

We are, however, given the occasional mulligan allotted
to those who have been there, done that. It is much, I suppose,
like the Champions Tour, where sometimes great golf comes
more as a surprise and where bogey golf is accepted as the
remnant of age.

If we are as fortunate as I have been and remain with one
media operation for a quarter century, we morph from talker
to thinker, at least in the eyes of those designing the playbook.

Perception.

The young cannot possibly deliver deep and well-
managed essays, can they? So they are assigned to the anchor
desks of our lives, reading teleprompters and cracking wise.
The old cannot possibly attract the young demographic, could
not be as hip and glib, and so they—we—are given the privilege of delivering perspective, offering the kind of opinion
that can come only with . . . hmmm . . . age and experience.

Of course, with a little shoe polish and some plastic sur-
gery, that whole scenario might be thrown completely out of
whack.

So perhaps there *is* a senior tour for us. My own gradua-
tion came in the early '90s, perhaps as much out of necessity
as of convenience, when I was moved from the anchor desk
to a more elastic world of . . . well, there wasn't a word for it
in those days.

"Just what is it that you want to do when you grow up?"
Bill MacPhail asked one warm spring afternoon. The god-

father of CNN Sports, brought in from CBS to oversee that side of the cable news network in its genesis, smiled when he posed the question. But behind that smile, there was a serious concern. He knew that I wasn't suited for the scores-and-highlights atmosphere, probably knew it from the beginning, but he had allowed it to ferment for three or four years until it had aged poorly.

When I left his office that day, I sat down at my desk and wrote in longhand precisely what it was that I wanted to do when I grew up. *If* I grew up.

I wanted to tell stories. My mother to this day claims, with a wry smile, that was my purpose in life from birth. I wanted to sit in front of a roaring fire, gather my friends at my feet, and tell them stories that would make them both smile and cry.

I wanted to place them on the wings of their imagination and visit people and places that would quicken their hearts and souls.

"Nice idea," MacPhail said as he fiddled with my paper. "Let's do it."

In those days, when CNN was a mere pup, it was just that easy. Anything, frankly, to fill twenty-four hours, and the sports wing needed to play its part. Within a few weeks, we had sketched out and then painted in full *The Sporting Life*, a half-hour excursion into the human spirit. It was, looking back, my debut on the senior tour.

It came, ironically, just as Tom Watson was beginning to go down his own road of reexamination. By 1983—at the age

of thirty-four—he had won his fifth and final major championship, the Open at Royal Birkdale.

He won the 1987 Nabisco Championship—which is
now the Tour Championship—and did not win again on the
PGA Tour until 1996, an improbable, stirring victory at Jack
Nicklaus's Memorial Tournament. In between, there were
141 fruitless events.

One-hundred and forty-one starts, 3 seconds, 3 thirds,
and 26 missed cuts.

Looking back, he obviously stood on the edge of a very
real professional precipice. Surely in those days, however, he
felt a return to victory was no more than a new putter, a good
break, a change of grip away. For a man who had won thirty-
seven times in the span of fourteen seasons, for a man who
had been the number-one player in the world for four years,
the slide to mortality must have been painful

If he had been given a *Sporting Life,* it is likely he
would have jumped at the chance.

That gift was all mine. We began on a wing and a prayer,
just me, a producer, and a cameraman, and ten years later we
didn't have much more than that. But in that decade, *The
Sporting Life* profiled 235 people and seven animals. It covered every sport from wrist wrestling to swamp-buggy racing, from championship croquet to homeless cricket. It
documented diseases like Happy Puppet Syndrome, brittle
bone disease, and Down's syndrome.

It began with the remarkable young LPGA star Heather
Farr as she fought back from breast cancer. A year after we

debuted with her story, we brought our audience her wedding, and a year after that, almost to the day, we documented her funeral.

She was our beacon for ten years, giving us the greatest of perspectives.

And the show gave the sports department a new phrase for its lexicon. Whenever they needed an obituary or a piece done on a struggling athlete, they simply said, "Let's Huberize it." Send it to the senior tour.

It was, frankly, a comfortable corner, where I was allowed my own pace and talent. I didn't have to worry about coming up with some kind of "Boo-yay" signature, no comical "Say hello to my little friend." I could be me, aging right before your very eyes. If my hair was going gray, and then simply going, it didn't matter. It never got in the way of Huberization.

And when I made the transition from CNN to TNT, remaining well within the family but crossing the atrium from news to entertainment, I was allowed to maintain that style and distinction. I was asked not to be simply a reporter but an essayist as well. Says so right there on the business cards they printed for me.

Yes, senior tour right here on the edge of the flat-bellies.

There is a difference, though, between my world and Tom Watson's. When a minor miracle occurs and great things somehow happen, it doesn't necessarily shock the world.

In the wee dark hours of a Sunday morning in August 1996, for instance, my home phone startled me awake.

"There's been a bombing at Olympic Park," said a breathless producer. "We need an essay for the network a-sap."

In twenty minutes, I was in the office, and in an hour, I had scratched out a two-minute think piece on what had happened and how we should react. It was on CNN's air within two hours and I was back home asleep shortly therafter.

Eight months later, I was stunned to receive a national Sports Emmy for that meager effort. Here I had spent weeks working on projects that received little notice. This production, however, which had taken me minutes, found glory.

I shared that Emmy, by the way, with NBC's wonderful veteran Dick Enberg in the writing category. Two old guys tied. And only I was shocked.

———

I sat at the table in front of the half-eaten veal and looked at my agent. Less than half my age and well-meaning, he sincerely wanted to negotiate some kind of huge anchor contract somewhere. He felt like that should be his goal in life. Getting rid of the gray was the key.

"I think," I said to him at last, "I'll just go with what I've got."

POSTSCRIPT

There are, tucked deep within the mysterious bowels of my hard drive, several books dying of neglect. In the near decade since my last published effort, *A Thousand Goodbyes*, I have fiddled and faddled with ideas and concepts, and huge conceits as well. Nothing worked, at least in the eyes of the remarkable literary agent who found my last one a home and then worked tirelessly to make certain this story was told.

"Too maudlin" was his abrupt reply to one.

"Mysteries aren't your style" came another rejoinder.

In the midst of those efforts, I settled for the very short story that television demands. Two minutes, perhaps three, concise and lyrical, words to match pictures or take the place of empty air. It is an easy application to me, and in it I became lazy in the ways of the long form.

Eighty thousand words? My goodness, I can barely scrape together eighty.

And so I seemed destined to settle for the one rather quietly accepted—no, make that largely ignored—story about my father's dying months and our relationship, a collection of dreams and wishes and bedside tears that soothed my own wounds. That and a slapped-together book in the midseventies called *The Babes of Winter* about hockey's emergence in the Deep South; yes, those would be my literary legacy.

Write another book? C'mon, I don't know if I have it in me. And what if I do summon all my mental juices and spend months spilling them, only to be hijacked and terrorized like the last time?

A Thousand Goodbyes, you see, hit the stores in the weeks prior to September 11, 2001. So in the angry, frightened dust of destroyed buildings and thousands of lost lives, my little tribute to my father came and went virtually unnoticed.

I have lazed my way through these years since, uninspired and afraid.

Until Tom Watson took my sails and gave them wind.

In all of my seasons covering golf, beginning in the late sixties, I had never encountered a man such as this. Because of his abrupt nature and cool demeanor, I had rarely given him much thought. While I had grown quite fond, in a professional way, of Palmer and Nicklaus, of Casper and Miller and Trevino, I had never come close to liking Tom Watson. It wasn't that I disliked him; it was perhaps more that I was leery of him, afraid to approach him. He seemed to have no sense of humor, saw life through flinty eyes, and challenged his questioners until they backed off and went elsewhere.

This, understand, was my perception. I am certain now I was wrong, unfair.

I saw that very clearly during those four days in July. I was blessed to be the first reporter he would visit after each round. Turner Sports held the American broadcast rights through the first two rounds and so mine was designated his first stop. In the freshness of the moment, we shared the exhilaration and wonderment at what he was doing. Because I was closer to his age than most of the other reporters, perhaps he felt I would understand what he meant by "special."

Off camera, several times, he looked in my eyes with kindness—something he had rarely done over the decades previous—and simply shook his head, the smile genuine, the emotion overwhelming.

I am sure all of us in the print and electronic media gathered at the 138th Open Championship probably felt we were being given a real treasure as he went about his remarkable business.

I alone chose to put it into these printed words, give it a spine and a title and somehow take a chance that it would not be interrupted by a jihad this time.

I would not have been able to do it without the great help of Watson himself, his agent Kelly Fray at Assured Management Company, and his wonderful caddie Neil Oxman. As I continually interrupted his work as a political consultant/caddie, he never failed to take me back to that week in July, translating his intricate yardage book for me, conjuring the memories of the best four days of his career. This book would have been a pamphlet without his help, and I will be forever grateful.

The legends of the game, Lee Trevino, Nick Price, Billy Casper, Fred Funk, Dow Finsterwald, and many, many more, could not wait to talk about the remarkable performance of their friend and playing companion, all of them gathered together for me by the Champions Tour media men Michael McPhillips and his successor Mark Williams, Dave Senko, and Phil Stambaugh.

Stewart Cink's memories were invaluable to me, and his generosity was all the more appreciated because he realized all along that the focus of this book, like most golf fans' memories of that Open, was on Watson. Despite having the coveted Claret Jug lovingly in hand, he knew that he would forever be linked with Watson . . . in the very best of ways.

I wanted to see Watson's heroics through the eyes of the one man who would understand and admire them more than anyone else, and Jack Nicklaus was overwhelmingly open and honest in his assessment and tribute. Through his agent Scott Tolley, Nicklaus recreated his own four days in July for me, considered the modern-day weapons and how they helped Watson, even gave me a critique of "that Michelle Pfeiffer movie" he and Barbara saw on Friday night. I'll leave that one alone.

My thanks to Chris Card, the affable new Director of Golf at Turnberry, who helped me paint my picture from across an ocean. How many steps down the back of the hotel? From how many places along the front nine of the Ailsa Course could one see the beach below? What was Watson's Sunday tee time again? What were the months like after the Open? When did they take down the grandstands? And the Watson, Norman, Price, and Cink suites? What color are those walls and is the balcony off the bedroom or the living room? On and on he answered, always with the brightest of long-distance smiles.

And then there is Andrew Stuart. I feel almost Dickensian when I mention to someone I have a literary agent. It sounds so . . . authorish. But from our first day together in the early moments of this century as we conjured the idea of turning my father's dying dreams into a book, he has believed in me like few others.

Over the ensuing decade, he has passed along ideas and I have sent him the stuff of quick reject.

"I know you have many books in you," he would say often, as if he were a surgeon diagnosing an ailment.

Nothing clicked until we settled on the amazing, poignant, heartbreaking story of Tom Watson and the 138th Open Championship.

If Andrew Stuart believed in me, Rob Kirkpatrick of St. Martin's Press took a calculated chance, and I will be forever grateful.

"I have no more words," I would cry to him often.

"Dread not," the veteran editor would return.

And finally my eternal thanks to Carol, my wife of many decades, who would find me at the strangest of hours hunched over my keyboard, deep in creation, and simply wander on, understanding the passion.

INDEX

Adams, 171–72
    caps, 171
    stock of, 171–72
Adams Hybrid, 18-degree,
    10
Adams Speedline 460cc,
    130–31
adrenaline, 201
    Cink, Stewart, on, 211
    Watson on, 250
Afghanistan, 136
age, 143–45. *See also* oldest
    man, world's
    Bean on, 118, 211
    Casper on, 139
    Finsterwald on, 118
    Freeman on, 112
    Funk on, 139
    Haas on, 117–18
    perceptions, 264–65, 266
    Trevino on, 139
    Watson on, 143
age limits
    Bean on, 34
    Dawson on, 258

five-year exemption, 259
Rose on, 34–35
Royal and Ancient
    amending, 258–59
Royal and Ancient setting,
    34
Watson on, 35
agronomy, 130, 132–33
Ahlers, Jaco, 25
Ailsa Craig (rock), 37
    local adage about, 37–38
Allenby, Robert, 7
Allingham, Henry, 162
Alliss, Peter, 200, 204
    on Watson, 170–71
amyotrophic lateral sclerosis.
    See Lou Gehrig's
    disease
Armed Forces Television,136
Armstrong, Neil, 170
Ashes, 25
Associated Press, 168–69
Augusta National, 251
Ayr Racecourse, 14–15, 25
    "ice patch," 15